By the Power of God

I am come to a time of life, in which it is not permitted that we should trifle with our existence. I am fallen into a state of the world, that will not suffer me to play at little sports, or to enfeeble the part I am bound to take, by smaller collateral considerations. I cannot proceed, as if things went on in the beaten circle of events, such as I have known them for half a century. The moral state of mankind fills me with dismay and horrors. The abyss of Hell itself seems to yawn before me; I must act, think and feel according to the exigencies of this tremendous reason.

Edmund Burke

The SAMUEL SHOEMAKER Library

BY THE
POWER
OF GOD

By

SAMUEL M. SHOEMAKER

WORD BOOKS
PUBLISHER
WACO, TEXAS

BY THE POWER OF GOD

ISBN 0–8499–2813–3

For HELEN
inseparable from the experiences
and convictions written in this book

Contents

Introduction

This is a book about spiritual power, and about the responsibility of the Church to make this power available for people.

Almost everyone feels the need for spiritual power. Whether we seek it for purely selfish reasons to increase our own peace of mind, or whether we seek it because of the need and deep unrest and inflammable dangers of our modern world, we need it, and we want it.

I am perfectly sure that spiritual help and power are as available to us as water or electricity. They are about us all the time, waiting to be appropriated. The air is filled with them. I am not talking vague "metaphysics" now. I believe that the help and power which we need was once and for all defined, localized, and channeled to the world in the person of Jesus Christ. When the Holy Spirit came, in fulfillment of Christ's promise, all that Christ was and did became universally accessible. Too many are more concerned with the formulas than with the results. Many in our churches say the right words, but do not appropriate or release the power.

Yet if God is behind all things, and has manifested Himself supremely in Christ His Son and in the Holy Spirit, then spiritual power is not only the most important kind of power but also the most pervasive. Some people seem to be touched by this power, some do not, some of us know it intermittently. I do not believe that this is primarily due to constitutional virtues or defects, but simply to the fact that some people seek persistently in the right way, while others do not. I have written this book in the hope that it may help indicate to some people a valid way of laying hold of, or being laid hold of by, the spiritual power we all need and crave. I seek also to stir the Church to its responsibilities and possibilities in this area.

I shall speak very personally in this book, sometimes about experiences in which I have myself been involved. I shall also in some instances speak very plainly, for I am convinced that the

Church, which is charged uniquely with responsibility for the manifestation and spread of the living power of God, is sometimes itself the greatest block to these things.

Taking a new parish in March, 1952, and moving into a new field after almost twenty-seven years in my parish in New York, has given me an opportunity to try and test anew some of the principles and practices that have been employed through the years. I believe them to be true, and the results which have come from following them valid; that there are not more and better results is due to my own failure to apply them correctly, and to follow them more completely in my own life. I have told stories about persons and groups because I think a pound of event is work a ton of wishes. Whatever I say of these people and situations will only be part of the story, for it will still be unfolding and in process when the book leaves my desk and goes on the press.

Every minister with his eyes open, every layman awake to today's issues knows that we need spiritual awakening at the local, "Grassroots," parish level, as well as in the larger groupings. The experiences and observations recorded in this book have grown up in living situations. If anywhere I have seemed complacent about results, please charge it to enthusiasm over people who have caught the vision and felt the flame—not to any satisfaction. There are people who have been missed, and there is work that still remains to be done. And if anywhere I have sounded too critical of the Church, put it down to the depth of my belief, the passionate convictions I hold, that the Church can bring the answer the world needs, and might be doing it ever so much better. I am completely satisfied with the sufficiency of Christ and the Christian faith, and therefore with the message the Church has been given to proclaim. I am completely dissatisfied with the fact that the Church is failing to measure up to its spiritual opportunities, in a day when they seem to grow greater by the hour. This applies more particularly to myself, and the things I say to the Church in general I say to myself in particular, knowing how often I fail to keep and carry out the vision I ask others to fulfill.

I must express my thanks to my own bishop, Dr. Austin Pardue, and to the Rev. Dr. Charles W. Lowry, and the Rev.

Sidney W. Goldsmith, for helpful suggestions. This does not mean they are to be held responsible for all that I have said, or would necessarily agree with it all. But they encourage me to print it.

S.M.S.

Calvary Rectory
Pittsburgh, Pennsylvania
April, 1954

Part One
OF SPIRITUAL POWER

I

The Release

of Spiritual Power

The people who believe vitally in God live at the right angle where spiritual power meets the facts of existence. We live in a real world—a world of confusion, perplexity, conflict, cruelty and the perpetual necessity to make decisions. If we use religion as an escape from this real world, we shall make of it the opium and dope Communists say it is. Real religion cuts down into that world, cuts athwart it in some places, but in any case makes it different. Faith works on facts, and either changes them or reinterprets them. The vertical shaft, for a Christian, is not one of idealism moving upward, but of the Incarnation, the whole principle of grace moving downward. We do not try to get up to God; we know that already God has come down to us—done it once and for all in Jesus, does it again and again in fresh grants of forgiveness and of grace. When we invite spiritual power in on our human problems, miracles take place. That is where all Christians ought to be living at all times.

Nothing holds for man so much of fascination, of hope, and of joy, as the release of spiritual power into his life and his world. We are fascinated by it, because spiritual power always partakes of surprise and newness, even though all the while we know it is what we are really seeking. We find hope in it, because our age has acquired more physical power than all other ages put together, and has proven to us beyond question that this can add only to life's comfort, efficiency and rapidity, not to its meaning and significance. If we are good people, we shall use physical power in a good way; if evil, in an evil way. As always, the real problem is man himself. Which is where spiritual power comes in, a power great enough to change human nature and so give us some hope about ourselves and our world. We find joy in it, because the experience of working with God, of letting God into our affairs, of finding that religion is a receptivity to God's action with us and in our behalf, rather than an attempt to hold always to a belief in Him and His goodness, is boundlessly exhilarating and singularly adventurous.

A great many people overexercise themselves in asking questions about who and what God is. They would do better to seek to discover what He is like by studying what He does, by watching the places where He has been, by tracing Him, as it were, through His footsteps. Nobody knows exactly what electricity is, but we know a good deal about what electricity does. We know most about God's nature through Christ, but this often does not become personal to us until we go into partnership with God, and enjoy the effects of His power in our own experience. Many will never believe much in God until they come in contact with others who believe in Him vitally and in such a way that their belief tremendously affects their lives. Many years ago a highly privileged young man named William Borden went out from Yale University to serve God and his fellow men in Egypt. While still young, he fell ill and died. On his gravestone in Cairo are the words, "Apart from Christ there is no explanation of such a life." There are many in the world of whom something like this must be said. Some are great, some are obscure, but round them is an aura, an atmosphere, which marks them as not just of this world.

Let us now consider seven different forms of spiritual power:

Healing of the Body

No one can have lived long, or attempted any of those experiments with prayer which constitute a living and active faith, without realizing that one of the places where God sends spiritual power is in the healing of human bodies. Probably the most important thing we can do for a sick person is to pray for him.

A tiny child lay desperately sick in a hospital. He could digest nothing and was going downhill rapidly. One Sunday morning things looked so dark that his father and I went hurriedly to the hospital; I made the sign of the Cross on his fevered little forehead and baptized him. His parents had many close friends who had become firm believers in prayer (they are told about in Chapter II). Alone and in small groups and in church, these people were pouring out positive torrents of prayer for this little fellow. Then he began to mend. Soon he was taken home. Today it would be hard to find a healthier little boy. Thank God for the excellent medical care he had. But some months later his doctor said, "It was only by the grace of God that we pulled that kid through." I know well enough that there are times when prayer does *not* work like that, and this constitutes a real problem that we must face; but prayer always makes such a difference, in the sick person, or in those about him, that it never does to omit it. The parents and the doctor and everybody who watched this particular child get well felt that here was an actual manifestation of real spiritual power through bodily healing. We can all have a share in letting such miracles happen, if we link ourselves to the living power of God.

Healing of the Mind

One of the saddest things in our time is the increasing number of persons being committed to hospitals for the mentally sick. We ought to take heart when we remember (1) that mental sickness is simply something to be faced and dealt with like physical sickness, and carries no stigma of shame; and (2) that a large proportion of these people are helped and healed and never return to these hospitals. But beside all that good psychiatry and its allied helps can do for people, there is also that which can come about only through the love and prayer and faith that are released by believing people. There are uncounted thousands of people who are unhappy, frustrated, defeated in some realm, and beginning to be emotionally or mentally sick. This can sometimes be reversed, and health restored, by the release of spiritual power.

A middle-aged man of fine opportunity sat in my study. He said he was full of fear and vague uneasiness and had a sense of uselessness. He was happy in his family, yet he was continually going off and getting drunk and making matters intolerable for them. Tenseness, inferiority, aimlessness, bewilderment, anxiety —these were printed on his face. I think sometimes people need a prayer treatment as definite as a physical massage, that rubs release into the sore places of the spirit as a good chiropractor sometimes rubs release into a sore place of the body. After he had told me a great deal about himself, and felt someone else knew and was carrying his burden with him, I suggested we try something.

I asked him to put his feet well out in front of the armchair where he sat, rest his arms on those of the chair and his neck against its back. Then I began praying release into him. I prayed for his nerve ends, for his muscles, for his bones, for his circulation, for his heart, for his head (he had said to me it felt as if a tight band were being drawn tighter round his forehead). Then we went to his attitudes, the thoughts he lived with every hour, the habitual residents of his mind, praying out the negative ones, praying in the positive ones, offering his mind to God to use and speak through. Then we went down into the cellars of the subconscious. We visualized our Lord walking down the cellar steps of his mind into these deep, dark, hidden regions where yet so much of human emotion, good or bad, is generated. If these emotions are negative, we are in conflict and unhappy. If they are positive, we are at peace with ourselves and happy. We visualized Jesus cleaning up the cellars of his mind, clearing out fear and resentment and futility and what Agnes Sanford calls "bruised memories," and putting in their place faith and love and forgiveness and hope and some new ideas. This took, I suppose, fifteen minutes.

When he opened his eyes, he stretched and said, "I haven't felt like this for months!" Then, musingly, "I suppose I am one of millions . . . maybe now I can help some of them." He was going off for some weeks of vacation just then, and I had a feeling this all might take a toll of his new outlook. But I was wrong. When he returned, he came in and sat for almost an hour, telling me what wonderful things God was doing for him and how He was leading in big and little things. One of his friends said, "It is amazing what has happened to ———. All his friends see the change." What many need is not a change in circumstances, but a change in the very furniture of the mind. Spiritual power often manifests itself in the healing of men's minds and spirits. Jesus was always doing that. And He is still here among us, and still doing these things for living men and women today.

Forgiveness and Reconciliation

Few things are so much spoken of in the New Testament as forgiveness. We need to be forgiven by God again and again. Part of the requirement, however, of His forgiveness to us is our forgiveness toward other people. "As we forgive those who trespass against us" is the phrase, right in the middle of the Lord's Prayer, which reminds us of this. Much of our misery and ill health could be obviated if we were rid of our resentments, hostilities and bitternesses. But these are not easy to throw off. We hate our sins for their inconvenience to us, but we love them for their sop to our pride. As many think they can easily throw off excessive use of alcohol or tobacco, *until they try to do it,* many of us think it simple enough to throw off an old grudge, or a habit of putting someone in a negative and unfortunate category, *until we try to do it.* Then we find we need a release of spiritual power from outside ourselves to help us.

A couple nominally Christian and ostensibly happy were actually very much in hell. His eye had wandered too much, and she was eaten with jealousy and fear that things had gone further than they really had. He came to be completely honest, and she to be completely trustful again, after a long session of candid conversation, tears, confession and prayer, and finally tears of joy in reconciliation. A year later one of them wrote: "A year ago we were in deep need. We shall never forget your saying that you felt there was nothing in our situation that could not be healed. Your faith in God's power to forgive and help us to forgive kindled new faith and hope in us. The year has been the best we've ever had together. There have been times of retrogression, and there are still snags on which we trip. But the miracle has been that we've always been led back to the right track. ——— has been more constant than I and keeps forging ahead even when I am slowed down. We start a new year today, hoping to grow nearer to God and to each other and to our fellow men. We hope the quality of our lives may express in some measure our gratitude to God."

Love and Service

One of the sure marks of spiritual power is intelligent caring for those in every kind of need. Christ set the human heart free.

There are almost boundless energies locked up in the human heart—locked up by shyness, by self-centeredness, by indifference to others' plight, by want of imagination as to how to go about helping them. Yet the world waits for the outpouring of that locked-up energy of love and caring! Some will never be helped at all unless *we* are so released that the maximum of love and care can pour out of us.

More than fifty years ago a young man lay ill on a bed in St. Luke's Hospital, New York. He heard the doctors whispering that he was very ill. He promised God that he would work for Him if he were returned to health. He got well, and was working at the old Lord and Taylor's store, on 21st Street and Fourth Avenue. He went often into my old church, Calvary, diagonally across the avenue to pray and ask God what He wanted him to do. One day he thought he heard Him saying, "Get going—get moving—I will show you what to do." The need that was laid on his heart was that of old and sick and destitute men who could not care for themselves and had no one else to do it. For a time he worked in a rescue mission in Pittsburgh. He opened the first St. Barnabas Home in 1900. He founded the Brotherhood of St. Barnabas in 1907, and it was recognized by Bishop Whitehead in 1913. Thousands of men have found love and care in this amazing place. The beautiful home in Gibsonia, Pennsylvania, with an annual budget of over $100,000, has its doors always open. The stories of God's provision by answered prayer—as when he had no bread for his men, prayed for it, and a bread truck broke down at the very gate, and emptied dozens of loaves out for them—are legion. The brothers make known, to God and to people, what their needs are. And wonderfully those needs are met. Their work is a monument to the power of prayer and love and faith and service.

Capacity and Energy

One of the perennial reasons religion will never disappear from the earth is its power to release in people capacities and energies which they did not know they possessed. It is as if somewhere there were an emotional blockage that constricted their output, as a twist in a hose constricts the flow of water through it. When the blockage is removed, there is a rush of fresh capacity and energy.

An insurance salesman felt impelled one day to pick up a pair of nail scissors and begin cutting on a piece of heavy parchment paper. His fingers seemed guided (for he had come through a real conversion to Christ, and was praying that he might be a channel of spiritual power). After fifteen minutes, he had cut from the paper one of the most beautiful heads of Christ that some of us have ever seen. This led to learning about lettering and illumination. The result has been that he now spends his whole time, and makes his living, by doing some of the finest illumination in this country. This power was locked within him. When Christ got hold of him, the heart and energies were released, and the capacity unknown before began expressing itself in lovely forms.

Have you ever wondered at the compact beauty of the Four Gospels? I have. They were a new literary form. Nothing just like them had been written before. More eyes have read them, more scholars have pored over them, than over any other writings in the world. Yet they were set down by men of modest education. The peculiar beauty of St. Luke and St. John is known to all who have ever read them. Whence this capacity to write the greatest books ever written? Again, some inner capacity unknown to its possessor which was unlocked by the Greatest Life Ever Lived.

In sharp contrast as to the importance of the event, but in the same tradition as to the way the power goes, is this incident. A young man found himself at a "shoot" where he was making a fairly good record. He was getting up into the top brackets in the meet. Then he began feeling "butterflies" in his stomach and it was likely to throw him off. He knew it couldn't matter much to God or to anybody else whether he shot a record number of clay pigeons; but he knew it might matter quite a lot to God that he should do his best. So he prayed, apologizing a little to God that the issue was so unimportant, yet knowing that overcoming internal fears and anxieties was by no means unimportant. And the "butterflies" disappeared, and he shot his best, and won the meet! He only told the story once, because he thought there was danger in praying about trivialities. When we talked it over, however, we agreed that the clay pigeons might be trivial, but the fears were not. We agreed, moreover, that if all businessmen like himself could find the answer to interior worries, it would avoid many an ulcer and many a breakdown and even many a suicide. All of life is

God's—the trivial and the tremendous. Nothing is beneath His notice—sparrows or clay pigeons. Nothing is too small to become a sacrament of His power.

The Spoken Word

It is significant that when an inspired Jew named John attempted to bring together Jewish and Greek thought about Jesus, he called Him "the Word." Jesus was the utterance of God, God manifested, God expressed in human life. I wonder why this expression was used? Beside the fact that it already carried a profound meaning, I think the reason may have been that a word is one of the strongest of all immaterial things.

The public spoken word has been one of the great means of reaching the world for Christ. I realized how useful our own English language had been in this enterprise when many years ago I listened to the great Indian Christian, the Sadhu Sundar Singh, speak to a Chinese congregation in the cathedral in Peking, through the medium of English. Think of it—the Gospel has gone round the earth not only through the medium of deeds but also of words. Some things in it—the Incarnation, the Atonement, the Resurrection—on which our whole faith depends, are not repeatable. We can only refer to them in words. We can only tell others about them in words. When the spoken word is in power, great spiritual force can come through it.

One thinks of the tens of thousands today who hear every Sunday the message of the Gospel in the preached word—and of the tens more of thousands who hear it through the words of great evangelists like Billy Graham, Bryan Green and Charles Templeton. The Word, preached with conviction and humility, is one of the very greatest ways by which faith and spiritual power come to people. One of the spiritual gifts which were given to the early church was the gift of "speaking in tongues," i.e., in languages unfamiliar to the speaker. This gift was highly valued, but St. Paul said it was better to "prophesy," i.e., speak in a way people could understand, than to manifest the amazing power of speaking in a foreign tongue unknown even to oneself. The publicly spoken word has been and will always be one of the great ways in which God comes to people.

The privately spoken word, however, may be even more potent. The word of personal witness to Christ on the part of one who knows Him may beget faith in someone else who has never been touched in any other way. Not long ago I met a man who has lived almost wholly for the things of this world. No one ever moved him till he met a layman who lives in his part of the country, who was once a pagan himself but who now lives by the power of Christ. The joy and contagion, the unselfishness and optimism, the fearless courage to speak naturally and humanly about his Lord touched this man's heart. "He is the best Christian I ever met," he said. That kind of speaking which arises out of living and moves from one life to another is one of the great channels of spiritual power. We need millions more Christians who learn how to do it.

The Changed Life

Perhaps the most striking example of manifest spiritual power is the turning of a life toward God in genuine conversion. It is also probably the most needed. Thousands of people in the churches as well as outside them need to hear the peremptory word of Christ, "Ye must be born again." Something so drastic and radical, so transforming and upheaving, must come to us ordinary folk that it is like beginning life all over again, being born again from above.

One afternoon several years ago in New York, I was calling on a family that had a loose tie with my parish. I asked about their son at college. He was home for the weekend. He came downstairs, not too excited to see a clergyman. After a few preliminaries, I asked him what he thought of the religion at his university. "Rotten," he said. Since I did not think too much of it myself, I smiled a kind of agreement and told him I'd like to discuss it further with him some time. "When?" he asked. I learned he was to be home again the next week, so we made a date. I talked to him at some length. We had a good time, but no dent seemed to be made. Either he was not ready, or I was not the person, or I had said the wrong things. I gave his name to some vital Christians on his campus and suggested they go to see him some time. They did. They went back—not too often, nor yet too seldom. They took a genuine interest in him, and slowly manifested to him the power and joy in a living faith. He said to me a couple of years later, "They came once too often, and I caught what they had. Meeting them has proved to be the most important event in four years of college. I learned more from those men about how to live than in all my courses put together." After college, he set out for medical school, for he had got far enough to want to serve mankind. "The only reason I studied medicine," he wrote, "was because I felt that it would provide a fine means for getting to the sore spots of the world." But then it began coming to him that too much of his time was going into technical work, and he wanted to be with people, wanted a chance to deal with them in more direct spiritual ways. "I feel underneath that the Lord would have me in the ministry directly." And so he soon entered seminary, with a fire in his very bones—this lad whom once I missed altogether, whom others won to Christian decision and commitment, and who now wants to put his life completely at Christ's disposal. Here is more than the difference between a student of nineteen and a man of 24; here is the difference between a man who does not know Christ, and a man who does.

Now that we have named and illustrated at least some of the ways spiritual power manifests itself, let us say two things more—the first concerning the Source of it and the second concerning the channels of it.

The Source of spiritual power is God. More particularly, it is God the Holy Spirit. In the some three hundred times where He is mentioned in the New Testament, as Henry Drummond reminds us, He is almost invariably associated with power. We do not ourselves either generate or create the power; all we can do is to channel it. Why anyone should ever grow proud of spiritual power (and people sometimes do) is a mystery, for it is so clear that man cannot of himself make this power. That is for God alone to do. The Holy Spirit is like a vast reservoir with endless quantities of power waiting to be appropriated. Let men come to this reservoir with great prayers and great expectations; the supply is unlimited. But let them come humbly, knowing that while the Holy Spirit is infinitely open and accessible to us, it is His power, not ours, that does the wonderful things spiritual power accomplishes in this world. Anybody can be the recipient of it. Nobody can be either the origin or the control of it. That is God's alone.

When it comes to channels for spiritual power, the field is unlimited in possibility. Anybody can be a channel who is willing to *be* a channel, not a director. We must not tell God what to do, though we can ask and in a sense may be allowed to turn the power toward some desired object or some designated individual. To be a channel, we must be open—open to God's will and plan, not set upon one of our own. Pipes for water, wires for electricity, must only be open. They are quite passive in their service. We, being persons whom God allows to co-operate with Him in His creation, are more active than they, but we must in one sense be just as passive in our transmission of what the Holy Spirit gives to us.

Sometimes the channel is an individual. A great pray-er, a great worker with individuals, a great preacher, a great counselor, a great personnel manager, a great mother, a great lover of humankind—any of them may be so linked with the power of God that it is God's power that flows through them to some beneficent end. Every individual ought to be an active agent of God in the field to which he or she has been called.

Sometimes the channel is a small company. Little groups of women who pray together (like one I know that has for years been praying for the conversion of the Communist Russians), groups of men meeting at breakfast or lunch, in offices or factories, become nests of power—nuclei that God can use the more readily because of the increased voltage that seems to be present when several who are "agreed as touching anything" (as Jesus said) come together.

Sometimes the channel is the Church. To the Church is entrusted that supreme medium of power, the Holy Communion, where so many millions of Christians have sought our Lord and surely found Him. Sometimes the channel of the Church gets badly clogged, and needs to be cleaned out, as I had to clean out some stopped-up gutters on my house recently; they were only potential channels to carry off the rain. But it is part of the mercy and goodness of God that the Church itself can be cleansed and reopened to the full flow of God's power.

In any case, in whatever form, to whatever end, by whatever agent, what sets spiritual power in motion is prayer. We can put our lives at the disposal of the Infinite God, and be used by Him for the transmission of some of His creative will on earth. It is a mystery, but it is as common a mystery as life itself. If all of us sought God, not so much to meet our own needs, but in order that we might be His transmitting agents to that part of life and the world which we touch, and this were done on a sufficient scale, there is probably no human problem which might not find solution. It waits only for enough ordinary human beings to let themselves become extraordinary human beings because they are as completely in the hands of God as they can be.

II

The Younger Marrieds
Catch Fire

The first service which I took in Calvary Church, Pittsburgh, was the funeral of an old friend and clubmate at Princeton. It was very natural, therefore, for me to pay a call on his daughter and son-in-law a few days later. We talked about her father in college, and about our first days in Pittsburgh, and before I left I said to them, "I think it would be wonderful if you would ask in some of your friends one evening, and let my wife and myself have a chance to meet them." They said they would be delighted to do it, and we arranged for an evening about two weeks later when the gathering was to take place.

That evening perhaps twenty younger marrieds came together. They were all of the most delightful and personable character. I had connections with many members of their families or friends and we had a very gay and enjoyable gathering. "Would you like to say anything to us?" our hostess asked in a natural way. I said that I should very much like to do so. And I began by saying, "I suppose out here in Pittsburgh you have some convictions about free enterprise." Yes, of course they had. "Well, have you ever stopped to think where America got her freedom? There is a Greek element in it, but by far the preponderant factor in freedom as we know it is our inherited Christianity. Toynbee says 'democracy is a leaf taken from the book of Christianity.' " We played that string for some time. They are graduates of some of our finest universities, yet this thought of the relation between freedom and faith was apparently quite new to them. I reminded them that the same Force that helps us to win freedom also helps us to keep it, by showing us how to use it responsibly and unselfishly.

All this gave to personal religion and faith a public relevance

25

which it had never had for them before. By about 11:30 P.M.
they were asking, "How do you get this faith you talk about?"
I said the hour was late, but I was good till 2:00 A.M. if they
wanted to go on. However, they suggested, "How about meeting
again?" We arranged to do so, and on that evening discussed ex-
haustively how people find faith individually. I related stories of
modern people like themselves, they asked questions, and we had
an interesting time. We met actually five times before I was to go
off on my vacation.

At the last gathering, I said to them: "I have three things I
want your help on. The first is, we need some more men to help
with the every-member canvass in the early fall. The second is,
we need a lot of good new Church School teachers: lots of you
have little children and understand them. [We got six canvassers,
and seven Church School teachers out of this group.] And here is
a third thing. What would you think of gathering together a lot
of your friends next autumn, and having a course for, say, seven
weeks on How to Become a Christian? Let us ask all the younger
marrieds we know, from any church or from none." They were
enthusiastic, and said we must do it.

When we first met in the fall, it was to plan for this course.
About twenty came, and we spent most of the evening thinking of
others to invite. Finally the names of 102 couples were suggested.
They were to be contacted by telephone in the ensuing five days.
I had prepared the seven talks during the summer.* I suggested
that we meet, not in the parish house—I was not out to make
everybody Episcopalians, and I wanted to reach the pagans too
if I could—but at the golf club where they were accustomed to
go anyway.

Between forty and seventy came each week for seven weeks.
I would talk for thirty-five or forty minutes, giving them some
real instruction and information about what Christianity is, and
how to get it, then let them ask questions. Each time, the questions became less captious and skeptical, more personal and genuine. The group changed somewhat from meeting to meeting, so
that we met a good proportion of the original 102 couples that
were invited.

---

* They are available in book form under the title *How to Become
a Christian.*

Just before our last meeting together, six of the men came to me and said, "Don't you think it might be a good idea if, next time, you gave us a chance to play back the record, and see what we've learned out of this?" I was delighted, and suggested they come in the day before to talk over what they would say. They did so, and I think we were all surprised at how much had already begun to happen to them. This was all their own suggestion.

Next night I shortened my talk somewhat, and then turned on these six men. By the time they stopped, their wives and friends were astonished at how much was happening. The whole procedure was in a very modest and humorous key—"Imagine a pagan like me talking to anybody, and especially this crowd that knows me so well, about religion! But at the same time . . ." Then would follow some point learned, some truth discovered, some experience begun. The rest took it up, till thirty-five or forty of them had said something. It was spontaneous, it was often comical, it was natural, and it was perfectly evident that God as He has revealed Himself in Christ was becoming a reality to them. They were beginning to say their prayers (some with husbands or wives), and to say grace at meals, and to attend church, and to try to live out their faith in daily life and work.

Then came the question: What next? I was soon off to take a mission in Texas, and for almost a month they would be on their own. How should we proceed? Most of the women had been attending some Tuesday morning talks which my wife had been giving on how to make prayer effective. They decided to form their own prayer group, and to continue by meeting each week and learning how to pray. This has kept going right through the year, and tremendous results have come from their steady intercessory prayers. (Incidentally, there are a dozen other prayer groups which the women have begun and continued as a result of those talks of my wife's.)

The men decided to study the Bible. In order to keep together, they began a weekly meeting at lunch downtown in a private dining room of the Harvard-Yale-Princeton Club. One of them studies a book of the New Testament and reports on it to the others, who are supposed to have read it, or important parts of it, during the previous week. It is a signal accomplishment to try to cover, say, Romans in three quarters of an hour. One fellow

said he was "late one day, and missed two books of the Bible"!
I sometimes go and sit in. But the point is, they are reading and
studying for themselves.

This group now participates actively and energetically in the
various church activities. During Christmas vacation, when we
wanted to have a bang-up Christmas party and dance for the college crowd at home, they assumed complete responsibility for it.
They decorated the hall, arranged the dinner, raised money to
have Slim Bryant's orchestra (best in town, they said), ran a
square dance, and had two of their members perform some wonderful piano duets of popular music. It was an evening the young
people will not forget. Their idea of a church party was quite
dim till they saw a good one. This group also felt it should not be
just an evening of fun, without a word about religion in it. So they
decided to let the young people speak for themselves. They made
me M.C. I introduced a college student from a group we had held
during the summer, and a teenage girl who had come through a
very Christian experience, and then one of the younger married
men, who told most humorously what had been happening to
them. This all took not more than fifteen or twenty minutes,
sandwiched in between the dinner and the square dance.

We have held a reunion of the group about one evening a
month. Some person who could give us a spiritual lift might be
in town and we would build it around him. One couple who were
great friends with this group were living in Texas, and we made
their visit the occasion of another reunion. One night we had an
old Yale friend of some of the group. He had recently been ordained. He spoke from his heart and moved everyone greatly.
Afterward, the wife of my junior assistant looked up from the
floor where she was sitting, and said, "I don't think I have ever
made a real commitment of my life to Christ. We were Meth-
odists, and I gave up drinking and smoking and all that, but I
don't think I've ever been really changed." I said, "Why don't
you make your commitment now?" And she did, praying very
simply and naturally in this group of people which by now, after
six months or so together, knew one another quite well. That set
off a train of reactions. One of the men, Dave, had been coming
steadily to the conviction that he must give his life to Christ, yet
he dreaded doing so. He wondered if he would stick to it if he

did. As he was talking about this, he caught the eye of a good friend of his across the room, and laughingly shook his fist at him and said, "Doggone you, Mabe—if I try this and fall down on it, and you ride me for it, I will be through with you for life." Then to me, "Can't you just act *as if* you had done this, instead of doing it?" I said, "Dave, if you behaved as if you were married to your wife, when you weren't, you'd be living in sin. You are married or you are not married. You are committed or not committed." He said he knew he could not leave that room till the decision was made. We were all praying for him, and at the right moment I said, "Why not do it now?" So very naturally he prayed and gave his life over to Christ. He is one of the people I can most count on at all times. The evening went on with rippling laughter, the deepest kind of warmth and friendliness, and the deepest expressions of reality coming from all sides.

That night someone suggested we ought to have a Communion service which would be an outward commitment in the body of the Church of these people who had made private commitments outside. So the following Sunday we arranged a special service at an hour when people with small children could best get away, and we all met at the altar. At the appropriate part of the service we said in unison, "And here we offer and present unto thee, O Lord, ourselves, our souls and bodies, to be a reasonable, holy and living sacrifice unto thee." It was a very moving occasion. We were grateful for a church that provided in its liturgy for a formal expression of personal commitment. Many will not know the full power of Communion until they come to it in a group that is already in living fellowship with one another.

One evening of the Lenten series I asked a man from the younger married group to speak. Very simply, yet with great conviction, he told the story of what had happened to him and to some of his friends. I wish that all the half-pagan graduates of our great universities could have heard it, for it was the word of a man who has got back on the track, and found his way, and can help others to find it also. He spoke on a night when I had very bad laryngitis, and we had agreed to have a reunion over at the house after his talk. I asked Dave, referred to two paragraphs above, to lead the meeting. He took the reins quickly, and said, "We have had a lot poured into us. What are we going to do with it?" Turning to a young lawyer seated on the floor, he asked, "Colly, what do you think we ought to do?" And Colly said something like this: "It would be very easy for us to go and find some kind of social service job, like running a Boy Scout troop. I think the challenge to us is to make real to our own kind of young people what has become real to us!" That is their aim and intention, and they are carrying it out in many ways. The next evening when I was to preach in a near-by church, and my throat was still too bad to do it, the young man who had spoken at our service the night before repeated what he had said to us, and I am told made a profound impression. When one realizes that six months before he was a Harvard University graduate who had little more than some ethical idealism (he had a great deal of that), and hardly any faith in Christ whatever, it was something to have him speaking in churches on two successive nights!

One day the bishop was telling me of having baptized the nephew of one of these couples in another parish. He said that it was not five minutes, after they got back to the house for the party, till these two had the ear of most of the guests, telling them what had happened to the younger married group to which they belonged. They never seem to drag it in, yet it always comes into the conversation. This has gotten pretty well round among their friends and acquaintances, and the lunches and tea parties and evening social gatherings buzz with it. Of course, there have been some ups and downs, some times of setback and discouragement. But a fever, a contagion, has been loosed among these very attractive, very sound, very privileged young couples, that perhaps goes beyond anything I have ever seen in my ministry.

There is not space to tell (1) of the way in which this personal faith is making a difference in their offices and the way they do the day's business in banks, law firms, manufacturing companies, etc., or (2) of the thirty-five or more times when they have spoken to other groups about what has happened to them, and the difference this is making in their homes and in their daily work. These would almost take another book.

I have talked with a number of them personally, and always rejoice to do so when it works out. But they have done a wonderful job of helping one another. I have never seen a group of educated and in a sense sophisticated young people where there was not somebody who tried to pull the thing down and tear it apart. But not one of these people has tried to do this—all of them are out to help themselves and the rest of the group keep going.

My bishop, Dr. Austin Pardue, says concerning this group, "The young married crowd at Calvary ought not to be an unusual phenomenon in present-day Christianity, but it is. The well-educated, intelligent, and sophisticated young people of today have generally not been led to experience religion in such a way as to make it natural, palatable, and personal. Here is an exception. This group are as healthy, normal, intelligent and full of humor as you will find anywhere in America, and yet they are willing to discuss religion as it relates to their own experience without pious narrowness or spiritual superiority. God grant that hosts of such groups may spring up throughout the land."

There are, I think, some imponderables in this story. Without something that God did, apart from any of us, I do not think it would have come out as it has.

Not long before this was being written, the Harvard fellow came in to see me one day. He said he had been thinking a lot about our next steps, and he came up with some excellent suggestions about one group where the men would continue to deepen their own experience and faith, and another where the men and women would gather every so often and bring in their friends and talk with them. He said to me, "I realize that this is not something of a few weeks, or a winter. This is a lifetime job. We are in this from here on out . . ."

III

God and a

Steel Worker

Not long after coming to Pittsburgh, I gave a talk to a couple of hundred men in our Men's Club. My theme was that I was not so much interested in merely building up a great institution in our parish, as in creating through it a spiritual force that could capitalize on this great industrial center, and set about to make its human relations Christian.

After the dinner, a man of about thirty-five came up to me and we began to talk. He turned out to be a worker in the Homestead Plant of the United States Steel Company, a member of a CIO union. He was gentle, hesitant of speech almost to the point of stammering, and I could see that he was deeply affected by what had been said. He had been thinking along similar lines himself. We talked then, and we talked later. I had no idea at the time how much leadership was in this quiet fellow.

The first thing he wanted to do was to help settle the steel strike which was then on. He had some very clear ideas as to what should be done. I sent him to a couple of our great industrialists in the city, who were much impressed with him, but felt there was nothing immediate that could be done. He chafed under this, but before long the strike was settled anyway.

He came to see me. "What do we do now?" he asked.

I said, "Dave, I don't pretend to know anything about industry as such. And I haven't any blueprint as to how this should be done—only a strong conviction that God is the one answer in industry, and we must get people on both sides of the fence in touch with Him. My suggestion is that you reach as many individuals as you can in the mill, make friends with them, open up on God and human relations, and see what you find."

Dave is trustful and takes you at your word. He set about doing it.

One night he was restless and could not sleep. He had been trying to get the general superintendent, the top heads of the company, and the union, to agree on letting him go ahead with plans for a weekly gathering in his department, where they would talk and pray frankly about human relations. He knew that this was the place to begin, but he also became aware, as he lay there tossing on his bed, of what the trouble was. He had been trying to do this great thing by himself. He got out of bed, knelt down and made as complete an offering of himself to God as he knew how to make. He took his hands off the plans for the steel mill. He stopped stewing about it, and just asked God to use him.

Then things began falling into place. In a union meeting, he got the floor and persuaded them to appoint a man to serve on a committee of union, salaried men and management. This committee stood behind his plans for the mill. His idea was to have a weekly meeting in his part of the mill, with a short address, prayer and some discussion. Twenty, thirty, forty would turn out. He would do the broadcast, or he would ask a Roman Catholic priest to do it, or a Jewish rabbi, or myself. Or he would open up on a passage of Scripture and they would talk about it briefly. This has been going on consistently week after week on Thursday mornings. Men have come into it from all sorts of religious backgrounds and from none.

But the real source of strength in this group seems to be (1) their confidence in Dave, and (2) the tremendous time Dave puts into individuals. In dealing with the union, he needed backers. One of the men whom he approached was a Negro. He did not seem much interested, and said, abstractedly, "I am in trouble." Dave asked him what it was, and he said, "I've got a wife in the hospital that needs a transfusion and I haven't anybody to give it to her." "What hospital?" inquired Dave. "Let's go along down." And Dave gave her the transfusion himself. One of the persons that voted with him at the next meeting was this man. Religion is as religion does.

The patient, persistent, loving contact with man after man is what has built up the group. There were two men who had narrowly escaped death in terribly serious accidents; their rescue had brought them from skepticism and indifference to believing in "something," but Dave helped to implement this and carry it forward into working faith. There was a fellow who was contemplating marriage, but was not quite sure whether this was the girl; Dave prayed with him about it, and they gave the situation to God. Later it came to him clearly that he was to marry the girl, and he has taken this new-found faith with him into marriage. Much of this sort of thing happened in an apparently casual way. Dave would find himself praying for some of them in the morning, and then unaccountably he would meet them somewhere in the mill that day and begin talking. A hundred kindnesses had their part, like taking the men to work with him in his car.

In a steel mill as elsewhere there is always the fellow who gets on your nerves and upsets the applecart. There was one— we'll call him Bob—whose job, as Dave tells the story, "is to take temperature readings of the steel in the open hearth furnace. He is young, quick-tempered and tries to be domineering to cover up a defensive attitude, due to his upbringing. Sometimes he seems to respect me, and sometimes he resents me. One morning about 5:30 the melter foreman began calling Bob on the P.A. system to come to No. 51 open hearth furnace to take some temperatures. Bob did not answer and I went in search and found him doing some other work that was unimportant at the time. I told him he was needed at 51, and when he did not respond suggested that perhaps the job to be done at the furnace was more important than the one he was doing. He slammed down the article he was working on and yelled out, 'I'll handle my job, you keep your nose out of it.' I said, 'O.K., Bob,' and turned and walked away. I was boiling. I had gone out of my way to teach him about instruments, rode him back and forth to the job, tried to be nice to him and overlook his outbursts, but this was the last straw. I said to myself, 'I'll see the boss in the morning and tell him I don't want Bob working with me any more.' I was really responsible for Bob and his work. Then I had to go out to the fuel tanks and measure the level of the tar. I was thinking as I went that I really couldn't say anything to the boss about Bob, and that as a Christian I couldn't stay angry with him. On the way back into the open hearth, I began praying, 'Lord, I can't hate Bob. I want to do Your will, yet here I am being selfish and proud, losing my temper, thinking of revenge, knowing I can hurt him if I open my mouth. Lord, help me, I'm sorry. Forgive me, and help Bob to forgive me. Help me to love and understand him and let him understand me. Amen.'

"I was away from the mill about four minutes and as I walked up the charging floor past the furnaces, I met Bob coming the opposite way. I turned out to avoid him but he came to me, put his hand on my shoulder, grasped my hand and said, 'Forgive me, Dave.' I don't have to tell you that we get along now!"

The process of quiet cultivation and making friends, dropping a seed here and a word there, goes on continually. Four months after he had begun this work, I asked him how many individuals he thought he had talked with in this way. Modestly he shied away from the question, "Oh I don't know—I guess two or three hundred." "Two or three hundred individuals in four months?" I said. "I'd hate to canvass the clergy of Pittsburgh and see how many of them have talked with two or three hundred people about God and human relations in the past four months!"

Certain men were already Christians, and these became a kind of team with him. Their points of view were varied, from Roman to extreme Fundamentalism. But happily people in touch with God and spiritual power, and confronted with a big spiritual opportunity, can find areas of agreement that are more important than those of dissent.

Dave wanted me to meet some of his friends. I suggested it would be a good thing if we brought along some of our younger married men, and we mixed them up together. On a Thursday night we gathered in a church basement near the plant. There were about fifteen CIO boys and about five sons of privilege in the other group. A really dynamic Christian experience is the only thing that keeps a meeting like that from being split by educational and social differences. The matter never arose at all. Dave's boys spoke up and aired their minds. One of them talked for twenty minutes the first time, and we just went through it with him; it was a kind of sermon. The next time that same fellow spoke it was for about seven minutes. He told three stories:

two about men he had been able to help spiritually, and one about a man with whom he had failed. He had grown immeasurably himself through the fellowship.

On the way home a university graduate said to me, "Before I was converted, I should have had little in common with those men, and found it hard to talk with them about anything that really mattered. But now it is fascinating to be with them and grow with them in this experience of Christ." This is of the greatest importance. If the Christian religion is to have anything to do with bringing together different groups, interests and viewpoints, something needs to happen to the individuals in both groups first —otherwise they will still be working only for their own interests, even when they seem to be friendly and co-operative. You cannot forge together two bars of cold iron. But if you heat them first, you can forge them together. Both these groups had come through something of a spiritual fire. Let me say in all frankness that this is very different from those occasional frosty meetings I have seen in Churches, where people of different interests and background are brought together "cold," and go away as cold as they came.

During Lent it occurred to me we should have lay speakers at our Wednesday evening services. Clergy and bishops are no rarity at Lenten services, but laymen might be. We chose five lay people: a metallurgical engineer, a great industrialist, an outstanding woman, one of the younger married men, and Dave. Some thought his hesitation of speech would handicap him, and he might not have enough education. But the thought persisted that he was to be one of the five. I asked him. He was pleased and not frightened by it—he said if it was a chance to speak for his Lord he would be glad to do it.

The day before the service, he brought me nine pages of manuscript which were to be his address. He was taking a course in public speaking at the university, and what he had written was clear and good. I was glad to have him work it out beforehand; I feared he would go on too long (he can be long-winded, like some of the rest of us!) if he did not follow copy. But I knew that it would be boring if he read it at the service. What to do? There is always a way. Before service he and some others of us gathered in the vestry room, and had some prayer together. The only thing that came to me to say was, "Dave, go to it. We'll be pray-

ing. You're going to be all right. Give them about twenty minutes
and then stop."

I gave him an introduction at the right time. He walked into
that pulpit which his father (who was years ago the sexton) used
to care for, and for twenty minutes poured out his heart. He
never looked at a note, and he never hesitated for a word. He
spoke a little too low, but the public-address system picked it up
and increased the volume. And at just twenty minutes he came
down. After service, one of our older women, who, like all the
rest, had been deeply moved by what he had said, spoke to me:
"I think you may have been brought to Pittsburgh just to set that
one man on fire." I agreed that this might be reason enough.

There goes on all the time this ceaseless contact with individuals, and the Thursday morning meetings. The younger marrieds
and the CIOs have met together many times. One evening, when
the numbers were small, we got an idea. Why not a conference
over a weekend together, where we could give more concentrated
attention to all this? We prayed about it, and it seemed just right.
We sought the right place and found it in one of the buildings of
the Pennsylvania College for Women.

We did not want the gathering too large. It was a training time.
Some twenty-two attended. Ten came from the younger businessmen's group; six from the Homestead plant; four were somewhat
middle-aged or older businessmen in the parish. Admiral Ben
Moreel, chairman of the board of Jones and Laughlin Steel
Corporation—the man who created the Seabees during the war
—was with us throughout. Friday night he opened up on our
objectives and spoke about character in industry and in life. We
went round the circle, introduced ourselves and got to know what
was in each man. We had a brief evening prayer. Saturday morning we began with a Communion service. Then we heard the
story of the younger marrieds told by two of them, and then of
the steel plant. Later Mr. Stupakoff, president of a ceramics
company in Latrobe, who carries on a fine broadcasting program
in his plant there, told us of his activities. In the afternoon we
played and met in small groups. In the evening we spent about
three hours planning our strategy for the next year. And Sunday
morning, after Communion at the church and breakfast together,
we broke up.

Dave sees the sort of thing he has been trying to do at Homestead extending to the other plants of U.S. Steel. He finds excellent cooperation from the men and from the management. "Yes," says Dave, "why not all the U.S. Steel plants? And why not all steel plants, period?"

Concerning himself he said to us at the conference, "I am the most ill-equipped man in Pittsburgh to be trying to serve God in this way. By myself I could never get to first base. I give myself to God every day, and it makes all the difference in the world. It has straightened out some men and some homes. We haven't made nearly all the progress we can and should make. But I believe the Lord has brought us here for a purpose. When we leave this conference, if we ask Him to use us, He will. Through us more will come in and it will grow. I know it will."

This may be a good place to insert something concerning vision for a city that came to me one afternoon as I was trying to rest. When I showed it to Admiral Ben Moreell, he asked if he might distribute it to all the employees of Jones and Laughlin. This was done. This is the vision:

Pittsburgh Is a Key City

It is both figuratively and literally "set on a hill." America is conscious of Pittsburgh. This city of ours could be such a leader as other cities might follow. It could set a moral tone in industry which corporations, cities and even the whole nation would have to heed. Pittsburgh is united enough and large enough to carry tremendous weight. If we here were to find the clue to an answer to today's problems, the world would listen. Stalin,* the Communist "man of steel," could be made to shake in his shoes if Pittsburgh, the "city of steel," were to practice a Christianity which is the dynamic answer to Communism.

Human Relations Are the Key Factors

The philosopher Martin Buber has made it clear that persons are only truly persons when they live in relation to other persons. We all know how important warmth and caring are in our home

---

* He was still alive then.

life. We must recognize how important they are in our industrial life. Men always want to matter, to mean something to their fellows. There must come a vast wave of personalness into industry everywhere. Businesses as much as churches ought to be islands of personalness and of saneness in the rising sea of impersonality and madness in the world. The human relations of business ought to be so Christian that a man or woman coming to work in a plant would immediately recognize the character and integrity and unselfishness he found there and would want to be a part of such Christian living.

Change of Heart Is the Key Word

We admit that our scientific advance has outstripped our social and moral advance. Material civilization has advanced while human nature has stood still. Dictators have tried to whip human nature into line with totalitarian principles, but human nature eventually resists. Christianity sets about to change human nature and often meets with resistance, too. We all want our own way. The other fellow wants his way. There is stalemate—or war. We like to think, and we hope that others will think, only of our virtues. But neither we nor they can escape for long thinking of our sins and defects. We are not big enough to meet the moral demands of this day and age. Our day calls for a greatness of character, for an unselfishness of spirit of which we are incapable by ourselves. We must change quickly and greatly, or we may lose our precious freedom. We have misused our freedom in order to get our own way, our own spoils, and have left others to fend for themselves. The way to advance is to face these facts honestly— we all need a change of heart. Only to humble men can God speak. Only through humble men can God work.

Prayer Is the Key Source of Power

We attempt to work out too many of our human relations problems without asking for divine guidance. Actually, what we need is God's help. Our forefathers gave us the key to the solution of these problems in the Great Seal of the United States where the pyramid of human society finishes off, not in stone, but with the eye of God. (See your dollar bills!) Our times call for inspired lives and inspired relationships both at home and in business. Only as we bring our partial and often mistaken viewpoints and attitudes before God, asking for His help, can we hope to know and teach the truth which sets men free and changes human society. We must pray often, by ourselves and with others, to find and know the will and way of God.

Exchange of Experience Is the Key to Growth

We need enough philosophy (general statement of truth) to get our sights set straight and high. But our chief reliance in the attempt to bring about this vision of industry in one city under God must be the knowledge of actual experiences gained from applying Christian principles. If we tell of our experiences, others will profit from them. We must learn how to share our failures without fear and our successes without egotism—knowing that it is God who works in us and who wills us to act in accordance with His plan, if we are able to place ourselves in His hands. We learn from one another. We must fearlessly make known to others what things have helped us, what things have hindered us in our attempts to apply what we believe and to do what we believe is God's will.

Application Is the Key to Spreading the Word

The Christian religion began when "The Word was made flesh." God became real. All that could be said in words, the Law and the Prophets had said. But what would be made real in *life* was not made real until Jesus came. He did not only *say* the truth, He *was* the truth. He was the Incarnation of God. With all reverence, let it be said that we must become lesser incarnations of Him. We must be Christophers, "Christ-bearers." Our lives, our words, our inspired acts, our deeds of honesty and integrity and unselfishness must be bridges across which He walks again into our world.

Someone has said that Christianity, like great music, does not need to be proved, but only to be rendered. The deeds which prayer inspires, which spring from a will to do God's will, the deeds we envisage together as we talk and exchange experiences and say our prayers—all are deeds that move men and draw them to Him who has inspired them. When we live as we should, men will ask living questions, and we can tell them without hesitation of our faith in Him. Thus shall the daily life of business and industry take on more and more of the likeness of a vast Sacrament through which God comes continually into His world and into our lives, to give them new meaning.

IV

Personal Hindrances

to Power

If this kind of spiritual power is available to us, why do not more people possess it? Those who come anywhere near having it know that it is the greatest gift and blessing in the world. Why do not thousands, millions, seek and find it? And why do many who have sought it end up with so little of it?

Let us set down some of the personal hindrances to spiritual power:

Being "Out of the Stream"

The longer one watches the emergence of spiritual power in this world, the more it seems as if God were always quietly pouring out a stream of very gentle power from Himself, all through the universe. He does not turn this power on full-force very often, lest it cripple and undo the freedom He has given to man. It is like a cool mountain stream into which one can plunge on a hot day. I have the feeling that many more people are *looking* at that stream of Grace than are *standing* in it. One can know and believe all the right things about Christian faith, and attempt to live up to the moral rules that are laid down in Christianity—but this is something different from being in the stream of grace and power. There are plenty of counterfeits of spiritual power. One does not know what it is like to be buoyed and carried until one is borne along, with full and conscious cooperation on his part, by the stream of God's grace. There is no "knack" here; we really get into the stream by asking to be taken into it, by plunging in through as full a surrender of ourselves to God, and to these waves of power that emanate from Him, as we are able to make.

When this happens, one sees human eyes light up, the whole personality glow and flame with power not its own. Such a person often comes by an insight, or launches into inspired words, or works out a situation in a new and unfamiliar way. I have seen them when they were so much in the hands of the Spirit that they became vibrant with the new life, and were capable of thought and word and action they never knew before. They are "in the stream." That often comes right after real conversion. It may come before we deserve it, and we may find that we have to work harder for the next gift of it, and thereafter pay for it through discipline. But the stream of power is always there. The tragedy is the number of people who have never stepped into it or, having stepped into it once or occasionally, will not pay the price of steadiness, discipline, work, and prayer that alone can keep them there.

A "Low-grade" Infection

Some people carry about in their bodies something that does not make them actually sick but just keeps them from real health: the doctors call it a "low-grade infection." Just so, many people carry round in their souls something that does not really make them cheerful and venturesome and believing, but just keeps them from real faith: it is a kind of spiritual low-grade infection. We get in this life just exactly what we pay for. These people, while they recognize that it would be pleasant and even wonderful to have spiritual power, know also that it has a price; nothing so supremely important and valuable could come cheaply. And so a great many people have just enough religion to make them a little miserable, but not enough to give them the kind of radiation and contagion which is one of the carriers of power. I often turn a hose into a bucket to water flowers in summer; it is perfectly obvious that the bucket will not overflow till it is filled and then some. It is a gorgeous thing to see that happening to a person— to see faith rise in them, just like rising water in a vessel, till it begins to overflow. What was dull and lackluster begins to come alive. What were just attitudes and beliefs become dynamics and convictions. Something moves in and possesses them that is beyond themselves. But until they open up their minds and hearts and souls more fully, this cannot occur. Nothing is more tragic than to see people, who might be enjoying their faith if they had enough of it, limping along with such a very mild case!

Want of a Vision

What keeps many from spiritual power is that they have so very rarely, if ever, seen it. They may think it way beyond them, perhaps a little abnormal. Their ideas of faith are formed under very conventional conditions. Perhaps very little happens in the church that they attend, or the community where they live. This whole matter of living faith is *catching*. It is caught rather than taught. When we are exposed to a little of it, we only catch a little. We need men and women of spiritual stature to stretch our minds and souls. Sometimes we can catch this by reading their writings, but it is far better if we can come into direct contact with them. So many of us live in a terribly small world, bounded by our own interests and prejudices and limited contacts. We are not fated to be small, we are just contented to be small. There may be considerable elasticity in us, if only we get in touch with someone who can stretch it. But it is appalling how we resist a big idea. Sometimes one pours out his soul in an address that is out to do precisely this—distend the walls of people's minds with a big vision of the world's need, and the way we can help to meet that need—only to have them say to him afterward, "You gave us something to think about today!" as if they could now go off and chew their cud forty more years, as they have done for the past forty! We need a searching exposure to a vision that gives us what Studdert-Kennedy called "a pain in the mind," asks of us more than we have ever thought of giving, either in work or in dedication, and seeing it being fulfilled in another makes us realize that the vision is binding also on us.

Self-consciousness

Nothing can cut off spiritual power like preoccupation with ourselves. We say truly that, until power is a reality in our own lives, we cannot let it flow into the lives of others. But we then proceed to take years to cultivate what would grow in as many months, or even weeks, if we cared enough. The truth is, we are mired in ourselves—in our little interests, in the shyness which makes us more conscious of what impression we are making or not making than of the persons we are with, and even in the long-drawn-out process of our own spiritual growth. "Out of self, into Christ, into others" was an old formula that expressed the truth about healthy, effective, powerful spiritual living. In a sense we shall always be conscious of ourselves—as problems, as instruments continually needing to be sharpened and cleansed—but then we must forget ourselves in the urgency of the world's great need, mirrored in the need of people directly next to us. Nothing so constricts the flow of power as the ever-present intrusion of self, wanting to shine and be recognized, wanting its own way, even wanting to possess spiritual power! Let us drop the old pictures of ourselves—both of our sins and of our virtues—and let God clean us up and set us on a new path where He can use us.

Fear

Fear lurks deep in the conscious and subconscious minds of most people. Sometimes it is a concrete fear—of being incurably ill, of death, of somebody's power over us. Perhaps more often it is vague and diffused, more like the anxiety which is present in all men and is perhaps inseparable from that spark which wants to keep alive at all. Some of us keep wishing life and its laws were different, or would make an exception in our case; we are in a continuous kind of struggle with the way things are which adds the fear of being overwhelmed to all the other fears and cuts the flow even of natural bodily processes, let alone those more subtle and delicate processes of the mind and spirit. If you are going to swim, there must come a day when you give yourself to the water; if you are going to live, there must come a day when you give yourself to life as it is, i.e., to God, to the outworking of His creative laws, to people. Thousands, millions of people withhold themselves. They have never entrusted themselves to *anybody* entirely. They seem to go about holding their lives nervously in their own hands. From the deep recesses of the subconscious on out to the very nerve ends of the body, there is tension everywhere. Stimulants to work, pills to sleep, maybe a doctor whose time we buy so as to have someone who will listen to our aches and ailments—what kind of life is that? Yet countless people live that way—really in unrelieved fear. It constricts the soul as much as the body, and no power can come through.

Solitariness

This all means that many of us walk deeply alone. With no one who can be trusted to understand either the shames or the aspirations of our lives, their depths nor their heights, we keep our own counsel, as we say, and live lonely, frustrated lives. "We do not want to bother others with our troubles," we declare, and thus rob ourselves of their help and them of the privilege of giving it. There is some easement and therapy just in a lot of women gossiping in a perfectly irresponsible way about their own troubles —at least someone else knows it. But there can be a great deal of help in letting one other responsible person know what we carry, where we are confused and need help. We are not lonely and solitary because we are not loved; we are lonely and solitary because we do not love other people. Perhaps, humanly speaking, love is the greatest loosener of spiritual power. The release of spiritual power is a profoundly personal thing, but it is also a profoundly social thing as well. Prayer is vastly stronger when several are praying together. The impact on a group of people is very much greater if two or three people, working as a team, strike together. Indeed, I believe even two people in spiritual fellowship create ten times the force of two individuals who pray and believe. The greatest single release of spiritual power known in history was probably Pentecost—and that was a profoundly social experience. We often find, and release, God's greatest power in a company of people.

Indiscipline

Spiritual power is not always predictable—"the wind bloweth where it listeth"—and we are likely to believe that it is subject to no laws. That, however, is not the case. For one real sign of spiritual power, there may need to be many hours, days, weeks, months, of spiritual discipline. We do not turn over our hand, and spiritual power appears; we work on the spiritual life, we study, we pray, we obey, and often out of travail comes power. Discipline in daily devotion, discipline in mastery of the body, discipline in the use and training of the mind, discipline in control of disposition and emotions—without these, spiritual power can only come in spurts and almost accidentally or, as I prefer to believe, as a generous "come-on" from God, coaxing us into something more permanent. Most people waste infinite amounts of time, of emotion and of money. Lacking one central passion, and the determination to bring everything else in subjection to it, their lives are scattered and undisciplined. They need a deep conversion to Christ, and then this needs to be carried on by growing discipline of life in all its areas. Long before miracles begin happening to and through us, the bills can be paid, the drawers cleaned out, the letters answered, the house tidied, the hours of going to bed and getting up and eating meals settled. One is appalled at the number of hours people spend in *just living*—shaving, dressing, cleaning house, cooking, buying clothes, etc. One feels they are often spreading this out because they have nothing else to do. How they need a great Cause, a great passion, and a resulting great discipline!

The Habit of Judging

Love toward people, prayer toward God, openness toward life—without these there can be no release of power. How is this cut off, then, when we turn from the loving responsibility to release power, to a judging criticism of people! This always does two things: (1) it fixes them in their sins or needs, as if the very saying or thinking of these things was like packing a hardening cement about their feet; and (2) it hardens our own attitude toward them so that power cannot cross the sill of resistance, and we make ourselves ciphers. When Jesus said, "Judge not that ye be not judged," I am sure He did not mean that we are not to face facts, nor deal with the unlovely and often evil realities in our lives or the lives of others, but rather that we were not to put people in final categories, where our judgment only adds to their fateful involvement in their predicament. We love to feel that we are smart enough, or "in the know" enough, to let others know by our judgment that we are cognizant of the situation. So much "judgment" as is involved in realistic facing of facts, we certainly must have, though we ought to keep it to ourselves, or if we talk it over with anyone, it should be with a responsible, nongossiping person who can help us in dealing with it. But so much of our judgment comes out of our own unhappiness and conflict. We lash out at others because we feel guilty ourselves. Judgment freezes, love thaws.

Want of Prayer

The deepest of all sources of spiritual power is prayer; and the greatest personal hindrance to it is the lack of prayer. I *know* that when I send up my aerial it catches power, thoughts, direction (according as God sees my need) from on high. I need longer times for prayer, especially in the early morning. I need to cultivate awareness of "the presence of God" at all times. But most particularly, I need the momentary, frequent prayer that simply calls out to Him a hundred, a thousand, times a day for light, for power, for understanding, for guidance. Sometimes it is not a request, just a "Lord, I love You," or "God, use me now." I have never got so very far in achieving a continuous mystical sense of God's Presence, but I have learned a little about asking for working directions from Him and receiving them when and as they are really needed. Frequently there is no great sense of God at the time, nor even of guidance nor power. But I try to keep the situation before Him, lifting it or the person to Him again and again. And I find that, when the time comes to act, guidance is there—I often do better than I deserve, or could possibly do without frequent short prayers. One can be clear out of the stream one minute, and back in it the next, because he is honest and asks God's forgiveness and calls on Him to be restored and put in touch again. Without prayer, lots of it, carried on more and more of the time, we can neither get into the stream of power nor stay there. None of us stays there all the time; but there can be a growth in the amount of time when we are available to God. Prayer is the principle secret.

Absence of Techniques

Nathaniel Hawthorne, in "The Old Tory," said, "Most people are so constituted that they can be virtuous only in a certain routine." We need some fixed spiritual habits. We need spiritual techniques. A technique in the spiritual life is a regular practice that has gained validity from being tried by others, and which we try in order to see whether it is the one for us. I know no one who has ever gotten anywhere in this field without daily morning devotions of some kind—whether it be keeping a Quiet Time in one's room or going to Communion in one's church. I find that such regularity as is represented in going to Communion once a week is provision for power that can be counted on; one does this whether one feels like it at the time or not. We ought to make a regular habit of worship in the church: it will lift us up when we are down, give us a new thought when we need it, steady us in the sometimes rather barren spots between times of great inspiration. I believe that Christ is objectively *there* in Holy Communion, by His own promise; I can meet Him there and He can renew my communion with Him. In the matter of daily Bible study, we need a method—perhaps a chapter in the Old and one in the New Testament every day. Many have found it helpful to keep a notebook and put down what occurs to them when they pray. The moment of insight is very transient, and we do not want to lose its thought. Setting apart the time each day, and the place, and having the books we need at hand, turns this from unrealized aspiration into a living technique. We need also to learn more about the techniques of dealing with people, of the ways in which God works in their lives, so that we can be better channels for His power when He wants to use us.

We consider these hindrances in order to overcome them. There is not one of them which is not, as Lowes Dickinson said of war, "a problem, not a fate." Turn them round, seek the answer to them, and we shall be on the way to power. We can be "in the stream" instead of out of it, find a "high-grade infection," an adequate vision, freedom from self-consciousness, faith to replace fear, fellowship instead of solitariness, discipline in place of indiscipline, love instead of judgingness, praying "without ceasing" as St. Paul urges us, and employing the techniques which others have found valuable. This is within the reach of anyone who will honestly seek it with his whole heart. God is more eager that we should have spiritual power than we are to possess it.

V

Qualities That Forward
Spiritual Power

Spiritual power has been possessed by people of every type under the sun. One has seen in a great variety of temperaments the presence of the living power of God.

But, as there are hindrances to the flow of this power, so there are qualities that encourage it. Let us consider some of them:

Human Interest

Most of us have seen at times a person of such great spiritual force that we were almost frightened by him. He did not seem to belong to this world, but to live habitually in heavenly realms. We may admire such a person, but he has what Henry Drummond called "theo-phobia," and we tend to shy away from him. If, however, he has a warm interest in human beings as they are, enjoys them, can get close to them, then we warm up to him and are intrigued by what he has. Jesus was like that. No one ever lived so close to God, and was yet so close to men. Children loved Him, sinners were at home with Him. "The common people heard Him gladly," which must mean that He spoke in such vernacular that they could understand Him. The more fully "normal" a person who stands for the things of faith is, the more we are inclined to trust him, and to allow spiritual power to get through him to us. One reason Frank Laubach is such an amazing channel of light and power to the utterly forgotten peoples of the world, whom he teaches his phonetic system of reading, is that he is so intensely interested in them. The reason they learn so quickly from him is that he cares so much that they learn. A bridge rests on both ends, and one who is to be a passageway for the Spirit of God must love people as well as God.

Faith

He must have unwearying faith. The more I see of it the more I believe that faith toward God is about nine tenths deliberate surrender, and faith toward people is about nine tenths believing better of their possibilities than they believe themselves. It is almost more a kind of courageous loyalty and persistence than any airy hopefulness about them. Faith so often creates the thing it envisages, while creeping misgiving destroys it. I suppose there is no one who is a tried channel of spiritual power who has not had to wade through sloughs of disappointment and disillusionment about people. Doesn't this kill faith? Not if it is the real thing. It tests faith, it toughens its fiber, it finds out whether faith can wait and endure and suffer setbacks. "According to the faith be it done unto thee" is not a counsel of perfection, it is the description of a law. When faith meets a tough situation, sees a person desperately sick, beholds the odds piling up on the wrong side, it does not go down in a heap. Neither does it begin to say that all this must immediately turn around and begin going the other way, if there is really a God. Faith just begins pouring out its own kind of liquid emanation on the person or situation. It starts softening them up. It trusts God completely to be able to bring about His will.

Humor

I am convinced there is a close connection between faith and humor. Humor is often a kind of humanistic, naturalistic surrogate for faith, and not a bad one either. For humor is at base a sense of proportion, as faith is. Moreover, humor is one of the ordinary man's tests for a person's humanity. The professional joker is no great shucks, but the person with a real sense of humor is a boon, especially when it comes to religion. Dr. Johnston Ross used to say, "Religion without humor is always somebody's funeral." In a wonderful little essay, *On Being Human,* Woodrow Wilson said that it is reassuring to see a twinkle in a reformer's eye, and we are glad to see earnest men laugh. In the amazing moment when great spiritual force is released, we may smile, but we do not laugh. Yet in the preliminary period, as we come into contact with people, as the stage is being set, I think humor—and especially that which is gently directed against oneself, is a very great factor in human closeness. Solemn people are not the best channels. Cheerful and happy people are. Someone asked Rufus Moseley whether he thought Christ ever laughed. Mr. Moseley said, "I don't know, but He has fixed me up so I can!" And he is a wonderful channel of spiritual power. Many have remarked that his humor is a divinely given offset to that in him which Baron von Hügel called "the strain of direct spirituality." Fun, wit, an apt story or illustration, will get you into the middle of people's lives more quickly than anything else I know, except prayer.

Compassion

I do not say "love," because the word has been so overworked, and, someone says, has come to mean "everything from heaven to Hollywood." Compassion enters into people's situations with them, and feels as they feel. It takes in the objective situation without passing judgment. "I know," "uh huh," a nod of the head, a grunt of understanding will often come into the conversation. People are often bewildered, hurt, shocked, sad, lonely. They almost never need advice or censure or harshness (there may be an exception here in the case of the hardhearted and the Pharisee). But all need compassion. It may be the very atmosphere in which new hope distills. The first change in the situation may come from our accepting it and them without question. Our own real caring may beget in them the desire to get well, or the faith that things can be different, or the belief that God Himself exists and cares. When people see faith, hope, and love all rolled into one, and coming at them in a stream of power and positiveness, something is apt to give! We shall talk with many who have never in all their lives been really understood and fully accepted. Oftentimes only a realistic person who faces facts, yet believes and knows the power of God, can be of much use in the situation. Love allied to faith and to intelligent understanding is filled with power. It must be free of sentimentality, and bathed in prayer.

Experience and Knowledge

A spiritual channel is not a purely passive agent, but is characterized by conscious cooperation with God. We do not simply become limp agents in His hands, but we put ourselves as fully as possible at His disposal for His will and use. Therefore, whatever we can bring to the cooperative enterprise of personal talent, of knowledge and information, of experience and tried skills, will be of service to God and to the work we believe He has given us. We do not want to present to God minds that are like a *tabula rasa,* but minds filled with as much of knowledge and experience about this world and about people and about the way things work in our political and economic setup as possible. So much of spiritual power ought to pass through the techniques of science, politics and business. That is, we do not ask a doctor to seek spiritual power outside his chosen calling, but in it. We do not ask a man in politics to be a spiritual channel in a vacuum, we ask him to do it *qua* politician. Businessmen are meant to use their daily occupation as sacramental means of manifesting spiritual power. Power comes in relation to persons, and especially persons in relation to other persons. The better grounded a person is in experience and in knowledge, the better channel he will be. If education, instead of being (as it so often is) a denial of spiritual power which makes the wisdom of man sufficient, were instead of humble and right use of the mind for the service of God, everything in life might become auxiliary to the better service of God and man.

Imagination

It has often been remarked that imagination and faith lie very close together. Imagination is a way of seeing what might be—so is faith. Imagination tinkers with the idea; faith believes the idea should be acted upon and can be realized. The imaginative mind plays all round a subject, like a person trying the pieces of a puzzle. It is always dealing with what might be, seeing what is not in place of what is. Some people seem born color blind or tone deaf, some with no sense of humor, and some without imagination. I am convinced some of this can be overcome. Surround children with music, and fun, with imaginative people, and at least a little of it will rub off on them. In dealing with sickness, or with people badly defeated in some way, it is highly important to be able to see through to this person well and victorious—not in such a way as to deny the present situation or to act as if it did not exist, but to transcend it in imagination, hope and faith. Imagination does not deal with unreal things: it deals with real things that lie just over the visible rim, waiting to come up on the horizon. "Anything can happen." "All things are possible to him that believeth." Both those statements are shot through with imagination.

Truthfulness

Nothing is more important, if we are to be spiritual channels, than that we be persons of deep inward and outward integrity. It may be right, in telling a story of spiritual power, to disguise the surroundings so that no identification is possible; the story itself should never be changed. Being truthful does not mean, either, that we tell everybody everything we know; there are many confidences that must be kept inviolable from even those closest to us or to the people who gave them to us—"graveyard," as the good old phrase is. But integrity means profound honesty. This is particularly applicable to ourselves: again, we may not tell everybody everything about ourselves, but let what we say be scrupulously truthful and up to date. Some can do a kind of detached counseling that keeps them in a different category from the counselee—power to them; I cannot. It seems to me the first step in rapport is to recognize that all human beings are in the same boat. It seems to me better to keep up no false fronts. And when we tell stories of what has happened to others—healings, answers to prayer, changed lives, power unleashed in business—let us keep only to the truth and not embellish it. Exaggeration is the first step to real evil in the professionally religious. How often have I seen it—so appealing, so plausible, "all in a good cause," etc.— but how devastating in its final effects of demoralization and the loss of power! Imagination can see all sorts of things; truthfulness holds us to what has actually happened. That can be told with all the gusto and verve in the world, if we keep to the facts. There are plenty of them without our manufacturing them.

Humility

We keep the most important till the last—humility. It is often misunderstood. We often think of the person who, in hearing the challenge to become an agent of spiritual power, replies, "Who am I to think that I can be used in this way?" That is not humility

—it is irresponsibility, it is funk, it is fake modesty. Humility never dodges responsibility; humility only knows that it had better not tackle a job requiring tact, wisdom, God, without praying. And, when it comes off with some success, humility knows that it was not oneself that did it: *it was done—through* him, yes—*by* him, no. One can be almost always in the midst of released spiritual power, yet ever clothed with this sort of humility. Some people give off, not one thing, but two things—not just spiritual power, but the consciousness all the while of Where and from Whom this power originates. When self-consciousness comes in, and much human to-do and palaver, indeed when one begins to assume that the power is going to be there no matter what, then look out—the signal is red, danger has begun. But the genuine transmitter of spiritual power knows whence the power comes. He prays, always with a little sense (I think) that this time it just *might not* come (Is this want of faith in God? Rather, I think, awareness of one's own sins and shortcomings). But then, by some strange mystery, it usually *does* come. We do better than we deserve. We let through something so far beyond us that we and all present wonder at it. And all alike give thanks—that is always the sure sign of humility. When humility is lacking, our first thought is of our having done it ourselves. When humility is present, our first thought is of gratitude to God.

There are dozens more qualities one might mention which seem to set forward the work of transmitting the power of God in Christ. Many persons are given special gifts of qualities which they ought to cultivate. All of us need these elementary ones. And all of us, by the grace of God, can begin to possess them.

Part Two

OF A CHURCH AWAKE

VI

The Church:

Ideal and Actual

The Christian Church appears to be the oldest continuing institution on earth. It has been called "an anvil that has worn out many hammers." It has survived the baleful predictions of cynics, it has survived the attacks of its enemies (never more savage than in our own time), it has even survived the support of its own members and adherents. There is something indestructible about the Church.

Twofold Nature of the Church

The Church has a divine and a human side.

On its divine side, the Church is "the extension of the Incarnation," the Body and Bride of Christ, the special channel of Christian grace to the faithful of all places and times. It was called out and created by Christ Himself. It was charged by Him with the care of His cause on earth. There is that in the Church which is abidingly sanctified by Christ, just because He chose and made it and deigns, in a real way, to live within it.

On its human side, the Church is made up of human beings, and is never free of their faults and foibles. It is often marred by sin, dissension, timidity and compromise. It partakes, not only of its Lord who made it, but of the fallible, sinful, half-converted, unconverted men and women like you and me who make up its membership. We who love it are most conscious of its faults: what would our Lord Himself have to say of it if He were, in the Psalmist's inspired old phrase, "extreme to mark what is done amiss"?

Some men spurn the Church for these reasons. They say the Church stands for goodness, unselfishness, saintliness, faith. But they find in it sinners, selfish people, unbelief and worldliness. They have a right to be disturbed by these things, if nothing is being done to try to deal with them. But they have no reason to stand aside where the Church is honestly facing its own faults and looking for its own change of heart; that is the company in which all sincere men themselves belong. We must not forget that hospitals, which exist to produce health, are themselves filled with quantities of sickness, and that schools built for learning must house positive concentrations of ignorance and stupidity. The Church is not for those who have arrived and are already perfect; it is for those who know that Christ is Lord, and want to follow Him.

Two Elements in the Church

I think we may also say that there are two distinct elements in the life of the Church.

There is the organized, outward, institutional element, which has a body, a place of worship, certain fixed practices, a tradition, a budget. We know nothing in this world of spirit wholly separate from body. "There would be no Bible and no Sacraments," said Luther, "without the Church and the *ministerium ecclesiasticum.*"

And there is the free, spontaneous, unorganized, spiritual element in the Church, which often lives in the Body of the Church but is never wholly confined to it—the effect of the living Holy Spirit in individuals and companies, sometimes breaking out in new manifestations of power and grace. The old, organized Church must be careful not to smother these green shoots of the Spirit—they, too, are an organic part of its life.

By and large, Catholics emphasize the first of these elements, and Protestants the second. They cross and interpenetrate at many points, and hold very nearly the same faith about our Lord Himself, who is the Center of all Creeds. When either of these two groups says to the other, "I have no need for you," something essential is lost in the total Christian experience. These two tremendous companies of Christians, loving and believing in the same Lord yet expressing their faith and life in such divergent ways, are witness to the fact that we have here two sides of a shield, neither of which can be omitted. Those Protestants who are currently in touch with the ecumenical movement have, of recent years, become far more aware of the essential nature of the Church on its Catholic side. From my observation, a like appreciation of the Church's Evangelical element needs to arise in the more Catholic-minded. (Someone wittily said that "ecumenical is the Protestant word for Catholic.")

The old, organized Church needs the new invasions of the Spirit for freshness and reality, for a return to first loves and first principles, for renewal and awakening and a rediscovery of the spiritual power that is often lost by sheer custom and routine from the organized Church. And the fresh and spontaneous movements of the Spirit need the old Church for balance, for historic perspective, for an understanding of the faith, and for provision of the regular "means of grace." It is difficult to keep these two elements in balance, but we must come to such mature wisdom and truth as is found in the statement of Dr. John S. Whale, "The Word and the Sacraments make one indissoluble unity. The Pulpit and the Holy Table, Sermon and Eucharist, are means of grace provided for us from the very beginning of Christian history."

The actual Church suffers from the mechanists, the idolators and the nonconductors.

The Mechanists

The mechanists are those who see the Church as a vast pipe attached to a reservoir of supernatural water. When you want water, you turn on the spigot. They see it as a system of wires running out from the dynamo. When you want light or heat or power, you turn the switch. It is a mechanical, automatic matter. Not only is access to this power through the Church mechanical, its effect is automatic. Go to church, make use of the Sacraments and other means of grace, just go and keep on going, and it is bound to do you good. Nobody, I suppose, would deny the truth that lies here. What we begin by doing mechanically may turn into something inspired, e.g., reading Chaucer, writing essays in college, listening educationally to great music.

But there is something else that can and often does happen. The exposure which is intended to awaken dulls and numbs instead. You can rub a spot on your arm raw, so that it takes in the killed germs of a vaccination. Or you can rub a spot on your hands till it turns into a callous. Habitual use of spiritual means, if it be not accompanied by inward moral and spiritual repentance and awakening, often rubs a callous on people's souls. That is why we must be continuously aware of the personal and subjective factors in all this. I can go to worship or Holy Communion with great regularity and seem to be making progress, but if I hold a resentment that I will not surrender or a fear I will not release— if, in other words, I am not always trying to open myself to that flow of Grace that I believe to be objectively *there,* in the Holy Communion, not only do I nullify its effect on me, but, as St. Paul suggests, I may be "eating and drinking damnation to myself." If all this is purely mechanical, then my friends who go to Communion with such frequency ought to display notably more power than those who seek to balance sacramental life with disciplined prayer life. Who can deny the often extraordinary spiritual power of the Quakers, with whom the mechanical is ever at an absolute minimum? God seems to use mechanical means sometimes, but we must never think that He is confined to them. When we shut off the other, freer ways of access which He often uses, we reduce our religion to a system. And Christ came into the world partly to deliver people from a religion which had degenerated into nothing but a system.

The Idolators

The idolators in religion are people who make secondary things primary and turn means into ends. Certain types of Protestants seem to worship the Bible more than the Lord of the Bible. Certain types of Catholics seem to worship the Church more than the Lord of the Church. Christ warned us plainly about putting the Scriptures above Him—"In them ye think ye have eternal life, . . . And ye will not come to me, that ye might have life" (John 5:39–40). One can hear Him saying just the same thing to those who have put the Church first. He appeared once in the world, without the connivance of man at all. He taught them about God and the truth. He formed them into a Church. To that Church He has committed various means of grace. He still stands above them all, using them when He will, dealing still directly with us, in mercy and in judgment, when He will. Some of us do not get through these created things to the Lord who created them. That is idolatry.

Of course, we can make idols of many secondary yet useful things. I grow very weary of hearing Episcopalians talk about our "incomparable liturgy" and Prayer Book. The Prayer Book never saved anybody. The prayers in it are perhaps the most beautiful ever written, but they are not prayers till somebody prays them. If we are converted enough to use the Prayer Book as it should be used, it can be a very great instrument of devotion and spiritual growth. But let us heed the delicious warning of George MacDonald, "As for any influence from the public offices of religion, a contented soul may glide through them all for a long life, unstruck to the last, buoyant and evasive as a bee among hailstones."

We are particularly liable to idolatry in the Christian religion, for the very central reason that ours is a religion of Incarnation, i.e., of concretion. Concretion may mean the ever-present temptation to idolatry. Many a man fearing and evading the issue and necessity of genuine spiritual power takes refuge behind the practices and massive front of the Church. Many fearing to express any spiritual warmth, or not having any to express, create a fiction of it in a pantomime of spiritual portrayal. This is at least once removed from the real and original thing.

The Nonconductors

The nonconductors in the Church receive, but do not give out. They are terminals, not junctions. Some of them are spiritual people with deep convictions. But one can hold convictions without knowing how to spread them persuasively. A great many people in the churches have convictions but not power. They have strong theological or moral beliefs, but these beliefs are noncontagious. Many clergy transact the Church's business, but do not transmit the Church's power. They are often solid, but they are mute. Or else, if they talk, they give arguments in place of evidence, and are not convincing. They have not learned to be natural and unselfconscious about their religion, as if all the while they were in the midst of a great and fascinating experiment and would love to include others in it. This is very different from seeming to stand on one side of a line (the right side), and inviting others to cross over from their side (the wrong side). That gets people's backs up. As you cannot get electricity through rubber, so you cannot get contagious spiritual joy and power through these dear old nonconductors, many of whom are loyal and faithful but do not interest the pagans and the outsiders.

Some of these people are "spiritual." Some have been told by others that they were "spiritual." Can you imagine Jesus being satisfied for anybody to call Him "spiritual"? Or St. Paul, for that matter? They were not concerned with this—it can have almost a "fancy" connotation—they were concerned with the release of God's love and power for His glory and the help of men. Sometimes the advent of this power was tremendous and came into clashing conflict with the existing religious institutions and leaders. These institutions were full of men and women who did all the correct things, said all the correct words, and doubtless were "spiritual" in many cases, but gave off nothing that penetrated the imagination of others and made them want the same faith these people held.

Do not misunderstand me; conductors do not always need to be great talkers. But they must always be great enthusiasts. Conductors of spiritual power are always aware of God, aware of what He has done and is doing for them, aware of what at any moment He may want to do through them with someone else. A continuous fire burns in their hearts. Humor and good manners keep them from being a nuisance, but it is always with them just beneath the surface. William James said that religion is always either a dull habit or an acute fever. Nonconductors have it so often as a dull habit, and conductors have it as an acute fever. You are always aware, when you are with them, that conductors are working at something, or rather working with Somebody. They are conscious of a Power outside themselves, never satisfied that they are fully in league with that Power, yet ever seeking to be more in league with Him. A person need not be a great pianist or even musician to interest other people in Debussy or Chopin, but he has to have an enthusiasm about their music. I have known people who could not turn a tune, but who loved concerts and the opera. It is not so much whether we average Christians reach a very high moral and spiritual ideal that interests and moves others toward faith—very, very few people ever reach that—but whether we care for Our Lord and His way of life, for the things He stood for and helps people to do in the

world today. Great saintliness is the gift of a very few; great
enthusiasm can be the possession of the most commonplace and
pedestrian person. And it will soon lift him above his mediocrity.

I see at least three urgent things that need to happen to the
Church:

The Church and the World's Need

We have time to idle, time to fight with one another in the
Church, and to occupy ourselves with little things, because we are
too little conscious of the crying needs of the world about us. The
forces of God, man, and freedom, on the one side, are locked in
mortal combat with the forces of materialism, godlessness, and
tyranny, on the other. It was a silly accusation for anyone to
declare that the chief pro-Communist element in America was
the Protestant clergy, but there was and is this much truth in the
charge: many if not most Protestant clergy have been little aware
of how a kind of liberalism has played into the hands of the
Communists, unaware of the great menace of Communism itself
in the world. We need to drink in these urgent words of Whit-
taker Chamber: "If I, who am the least man in this nation, which
is dying of self-satisfaction and indifference—if I do not find
within myself the strength to do this, then, in the war between
this world and Communism which is inevitably coming, any man
will have the moral right to ask, 'Why should I give my life'? But
if I do find this strength, nothing, ultimately, can destroy this
nation, for it is the power of souls to move other souls."

Much of the world's need is for food and for knowledge.
Enough knowledge has leaked through to the world's illiterates
and desperates for them to know they need not remain ignorant,
sick and hungry. The Christian Church must spearhead the movement to help these people help themselves. Dr. Frank Laubach's
vision of a "war of amazing kindness" has many expressions, one
of which is what we call World Neighbors, which is out to secure
twenty millions of privately given money for this work. It is not
enough for the Church to propagate its faith in words; it must
sacramentalize its faith in deeds.

It is fatal to think all the danger is on the other side of the Iron
Curtain. In many places, paganism is eating the heart out of
America. What we spend on foolish and needless luxury would

almost lift the world's population to a new level. This nation spends some seven billion annually on tobacco, and eight billion on liquor. But we spend about $1.50 per head per annum out of each $100 for the Church and welfare institutions. There is a Christian America, and there is a pagan America. The country will not continue half-Christian, half-pagan. Something is going to win. Which is it going to be?

A Truer View of Sin

When we say "sin" in Church, many turn away in disgust. Part of this is due to the preoccupation of church people with petty sins. It is not petty when one is resentful, or bedeviled with alcohol, or defeated by fear, but it is petty when all this is seen only in connection with personal improvement. Our great sin is living in such a small world, and traveling at such a snail's pace. We are not so much wicked as ineffective, complacent, and unutterably slow. Nine tenths of what the Church is doing today is so irrelevant in the world scene that it constitutes a kind of treason. I know people who have been in the Church for years who, when you ask them to try to get their faith over to someone else, say, "Oh I am not ready for that; I must learn more about Christianity." What have they been doing for ten, twenty, forty years? St. Paul foresees as one of the groups causing trouble in the Church (2 Tim. 3:7) those who are "ever learning and never able to come to a knowledge of the truth." This does not represent honest humility; this represents shameful delay and irresponsibility. The greatest sin of us Christians is not our sins of passion, or our less obvious sins of attitude. It is our woeful ineffectiveness in the presence of so much unmet need, when we have access to so much power. We shall see the little and personal problems in their true light when we see the sum of them hanging like a millstone round our necks, and holding us back from being and doing what we should.

A More Inspired Leadership

Are we training men for the Church's leadership who think and feel and act in this way? Some, I hope. But certainly not enough. The usual three years of seminary are curiously unlike the three years' preparation Jesus gave the apostles. He did not withdraw them from the world for concentrated study of religion. He took them with Him as He went to individuals and groups and places and carried spiritual power directly to them. Something more than Christian conversion and their call to the ministry is needed if these men are to be trained. But why does all the technical training so often dull the edge of conviction? Why do I see fairly mature men come into seminaries, sometimes from having done other work in the world, only to have their want of technical knowledge met by such immersion in theological profundities and the customs and habits of professional Christians that they often come out dehumanized, remote from life, carrying round with them for a time an ivory-tower encasment which is only slowly shed? Says a man who knows what he's talking about, though he is a young minister: "People need a lot of time and a vision. I get disturbed with some of the boys going into the ministry who have no vision of going out and winning men to Christ." These men need to learn how to get people in touch with the power of God through genuine conversion, and how to form them into centers of radiant influence among their fellows. A great many men in seminary are going to psychiatrists. I have nothing whatever against psychiatrists, and I work with them often—undoubtedly some men in seminaries do need their help. But if the seminaries were themselves Churches and not mere graduate schools, if the instructors were giving to the men the same kind of spiritual care as they are intended later to give to their own people, I think there would be far less need of psychiatric help. You say the professors do not have enough time for this? Jesus found time for it, and He had the salvation of the world on His hands. He did not send people out to tell what the Gospel was, but to manifest its power in action. So many of our clergy can tell you what it is, but not so many can channel its power in persuasive ways. Many of the men I meet in seminaries are like nothing so much as little boys playing church. Our people do not live enough like the people in the New Testament. Our bishops and clergy do not behave enough like the apostles and early disciples. We have dropped into a lower key, declined to a cheaper level, become content with a poorer product, and are willing to settle for entirely too little when it comes to experience. There is a seething discontent with seminaries on the part of many bishops and other church authorities whom I know. One has the feeling that men are being taught much about the early Church—almost everything, except the truth George Fox saw and expressed that "none are successors to the Prophets and Apostles, but who succeed them in the same power and Holy Ghost that they were in."

VII

The Church and

Awakening

I think there is no doubt in the mind of any believing Christian that Jesus Christ is not only the world's one hope but also the world's one way. We know that in Him there is sufficient power to meet any problem, transcend any tragedy and meet any opportunity that will ever face us. We know that, though we cannot use those means of coercion and corruption which the Communists have used to persuade men by the millions to their way of thinking, the ways of spiritual power are much more ingenious and welcome, and ought to be much more effective, than the ways of tyranny and domination. We find ourselves dismayed, as Christians, at being unable to bring to the world effectively and in time the answer of its only hope.

Our need, therefore, is for something that will open up the channel of the Church itself to carry more power and convey her message more widely. Nothing, we believe, is lacking in the message—the message is the Lord Jesus Himself. I do not think that so very much is lacking in our grasp of the intellectual meaning of the message. Our new concern for theology and return in recent years to much deeper views both of the Bible and of the Church have moved us from our shaky ethical position to the real thing we have to proclaim, i.e., the coming of God to earth in Jesus for man's full redemption. The defect, as we have said, is in the human part of the Church. It is in us. We do not channel the full power of the Gospel because we do not sufficiently let that power lay hold of us. Better instruments would be better channels.

Everyone even remotely connected with the Church knows that our great need, in every church, in every land, is spiritual awakening. It is fashionable and "good form" to say this now—even to use the word "evangelism" which did not have a savory taste a few years ago. The prospectus of the Second Assembly of the World Council of Churches says, "Evangelism is a popular word and subject, increasingly recognized to be the primary function of the Church and the chief work of the Christian." Our leaders say things like this. I am not sure how much they mean them, for, after paying lip service to this ideal and dream, many of them turn immediately from it to the pursuit of the same old thing in the same old way. They ought to stop to decide on their knees that the conversion of the Church is now and always the Church's first business. We shall not be used to convey the message to others till we have let it invade and captivate us. The truth is, no one of us is converted till we are eager and ready to pass on to other people what has made so much difference to us.

The average Christian begs off from this—clergy as well as lay person. We say this is a thing for experts, and will not get down to the fact that evangelism can be caught and learned from people who are doing it. Right under our noses the movement called Alcoholics Anonymous tells all its people they must go on to "Twelfth Step Word," and pass on to other alcoholics what has come to them. By hearing many stories of "recovered" men and women, they get the "hang" of it; they learn a kind of theology and a kind of psychology. Our excuses, as churchmen, look very lame by comparison. The truth is that our own spiritual experience is often so hazy, so lacking in acuteness and concreteness, that we are afraid to launch out into a discussion in which eventually we shall be thrown back on the simple witness of our own experience. We know only too well there is not very much of it there! No wonder the Archbishops' Report (called "Towards the Conversion of England") said, "The Church is at present itself a field for evangelism rather than a force for evangelism," and "a large proportion of worshippers are only half-converted."

The clergy and leaders of our more educated communions find themselves more congenially employed in attempting to nurture and educate those who have been initially won by others. It is easier to press gently upon people the Church's ways of growth than to press upon them with conviction the challenge of conversion to Christ. What is usually called "nurture" is offered to people whose initial interest in religion is so unawakened that this is putting the cart before the horse. The persons supposed to be in this process are simply those who like to go to Church and sing hymns, but who often have no idea of changing in any deep way. The plain fact is that doing what we are doing now, or merely doing more of the same thing, will cause us to fail God and our generation. We trust too much to the inherent reasonableness of the Gospel to carry itself, with insufficient effort at the persuasion that results in decision. We do not have the contagion of a great and lasting enthusiasm, which is always the catching spark of faith. We are earnest and sincere and instructed, perhaps, but we are not on fire. We are not daily and hourly accustomed to expecting and seeing conversions and other manifestations of spiritual power, and being used by God to bring them about. If they happen at all, they happen rarely. And we are rather proud of our humility when we say, "Some have the gift, but I have to work in more quiet ways." "O so quiet," says Bryan Green in commenting on some clergy.

Some of us have not got so far as to be converted; we have only been a little civilized by our religion. And this means that we are terribly allergic to what we think are rude or crude kinds of evangelism. Some have sought the protection of the more educated communions to "get away" from emotional religion that is in bad taste. I do not think that evangelism ever needs to transgress good manners, though a living evangelism will always upset some people. I am sure Jesus was never bad-mannered, though He often spoke and acted in ways that offended the spiritually smug. Some people in the "standard-brand" churches would settle for a nice, intelligent, well-bred variety of Presbyterian or Anglican or other evangelism if they could find it, but they start out by giving notice to the Holy Spirit that all this must conform to their own specifications. I wonder what some of these dear people would have done with Pentecost! I am sure they would have said it was dangerously emotional and likely to get out of hand. We approach all this in such a terribly theoretical way that we do not at all know what goes into evangelism, and the producing of conversions, and new life in people. It is as if we said it is a wonderful thing to keep up the birth rate, and a glorious experi-

ence personally to have children—we love the little things all
wrapped up in pink or blue in their cribs—but why must there
be these cries and this pain and this blood and danger in the
hospital when they are born? This does not daunt a good doctor,
but sometimes the inexperienced faint. We have all too few
spiritual doctors who know anything at all about bringing people
through the "second birth." To be all in favor of the general idea
is quite different from being able to bring about new life in one
human soul.

We think that one way to achieve what we need is to depart-
mentalize it, and call in a specialist. The Church has always had
some striking preachers with an evangelical message—Whitefield,
the Wesleys, Finney, Moody, Sunday—and in our time especially
the two B. G.'s—Billy Graham and Bryan Green. My experience
with the last two is that they do a most excellent job. They touch
people inside and outside the churches who find something that
moves their hearts in the strong appeals to discipleship and
decision which these men put before their hearers. But what next?

The second stage is the necessity of follow-up by local religious
groups. And that is where we find much of the reason that the
campaign may be an indifferent success with mediocre results.
The names are sent in, the local clergy often do a good job of
looking the people up and attempting to relate them to the
Church. But the churches are not guaged to these new converts,
but rather to those already domesticated within them. They are
not like families of the age of twenty-five to thirty-five with new
children coming in; they are like families of the age of fifty to
sixty-five. I am not speaking of the want of *young* people, but of
the want of *recently converted* people. Men who do not themselves bring about conversions as a result of their own work are
likely to be inept at conserving the results brought about by
others, as maiden aunts do not make such good nurses as mothers
do. The ministers and people of many of our churches are accustomed to accessions, but not to conversions; these may, but
also may not, coincide. They have little idea of what happens in
a deep conversion, or of how it is continued and sustained: often
all they can do is to draw these people into the dull and lackluster activities of the church, where they miss the joy and contagion of the original impulse that won them for Christ. Someone

said that you can't put a live chick under a dead hen. And as for evangelism, and the knowledge of how to win people decisively for Christ, many a church is honestly a "dead hen."

I remember in China many years ago, when Sherwood Eddy was holding an evangelistic campaign, a fine young Chinese student made a Christian decision. The only missionary he knew was an English bishop. He went to see him. The bishop, somewhat distrustful of conversions, began to instruct the young man in the orderly and common-sense ways of the Church, forgot that he needed fellowship and continued inspiration, gave him a little stiff book of Confirmation, in which the student discovered that in England the King has most to do with the appointment of bishops. Upon which he went roaring into the Methodist Church! That's a very good place to go, but I do not think the good bishop's dealing with a new convert manifested the greatest understanding of what he needed. You know well that for a new convert to adapt himself to the low level of spiritual life and evangelism that characterizes most parishes would be almost to forget his conversion. How much better if we drew in many more new and converted people, and then adapted the often prosy, institutional, uninspired ways of the Church to meet the needs of the new converts!

There is another thing. For those in comfortable, settled places, and for the Church's bureaucrats who shuttle between desks and suitcases, the manifestation of genuine spiritual power of an evangelistic kind produces very mixed emotions. Awakening is all right (they say), but can we be sure all this will be channeled right into the Church again, and especially into *my* Church? Will not these new converts give a kind of loyalty to the men God used to convert them, rather than to the settled clergy who failed to do it? This produces a kind of threat. "These men who have turned the world upside down have come here also." And thereupon one of two things happens: (1) either the more regular-issue men who may have prayed for an awakening in general but did not quite expect God to send it to them in just this form or at just this time have the grace to admit that this holds for them the challenge of doing more vital and dynamic work with people; or (2) there begins an opposition to these disturbing people which may be subtle and underground, or may be open and manifest.

We should love to have awakening come in general, or to the other fellow, but when awakening starts in growing pains for ourselves, and in the admission that our hordes of committees are no substitute for vital dealing with souls, that we are fooling ourselves about real results and that much of our monetary and membership success is as thin as the paper on the wall—then we begin to grow uneasy. The first step in true awakening is a fresh conviction of sin—*my* sin. This applies just as much to us who may have been Christians for years as to those who are just beginning to find their Lord. The growing pains are hard and unwelcome. When they seem to reflect at all on the level of our lives and ministries, we just say this is going too far, and want to be rid of the whole matter, including the men who were used to lay these uncomfortable ideas in our laps. From the New Testament to John Wesley, and from John Wesley till now, this has been the all too familiar pattern. Painless awakening we should like; costly, painful awakening—no. Luther said, "When human creatures will reform the church, then it costs blood."

We probably can never estimate how many times the Holy Spirit has prepared a man or group who were settled in their determination to give themselves to God for the work of awakening, only to have the organized Church throw cold water on the fires and put them out, seeing more danger than promise in the new manifestation. Indeed some *have* been dangerous, in content and in method, and were to be eschewed. But often they have not been eschewed because they were invalid, but because they were uncomfortable—because they were "dangerous," not in being faithless to Christ and the Church, but because they challenged so much that goes on officially in the name of Christ and the Church.

It has happened again recently. Three very promising young men, recent seminary graduates, duly ordained in their own communion, banded themselves together to operate in an informal and very effective way on college campuses. I have watched them at work many times, and consider them to have as great a talent for reaching students spiritually as any men I ever met. They touched hundreds and hundreds in the twenty-five or so colleges which they visited. Many of these young people say openly that this was the first thing that ever really awakened them to Christ, and some of these young people were connected with churches. I have watched their approach—the almost perfect point of contact, the humorous, deep presentation of the Gospel in the vernacular (which is the way Christ Himself spoke), the flow of countless stories of individual boys and girls for whom the experience of Christ had become a reality, the flood of personal interviews taking every waking hour they had (the most exhausting and rewarding kind of self-giving imaginable), and great conversions got under way which must be left to the local religious authorities to conserve and nurture. This was done in complete loyalty to the Church's historic faith. It was done in the fullest possible cooperation with the existing forces of their own and other churches on the campuses. It was done in a spirit of entire teachableness, admitting mistakes when they were made, and open to new truth and procedures, which of course did not extend to heeding the counsels of those who themselves do nothing about direct evangelistic work.

A lawyer, a layman, who knows their work at first hand and has seen it in operation says of them, "I have seen it work. . . . The results are unbelievable, effects incalculable. I have seen heterogeneous, diverse temperaments, intellects, personalities, held together in big bull sessions—important bull sessions, where the subject under discussion is the most important subject in the world. I have seen these boys lead groups in prayer, seen these groups transformed into single, devout and prayerful units. I have seen dissension, argument, intellectual sophistry, intellectual pride and arrogance swept away by the Holy Spirit. I have seen and felt that Spirit flood in through a college group with tidal intensity, and the personality of each person in the room suffused with virtually indescribable experience. . . . The creative approach of this group is nothing short of a crusade, a new weapon to bring to a highly educated group the realization of the great and tender miracle of the Love of God in Jesus Christ."

Yet the committee of their communion charged with responsibility for these things withdrew all support after only a year's trial. And these were the grounds:

1. "Apprehension concerning possible involvement in an independent evangelistic movement apart from the Church." (How often, I should like to know, has an official church body begun

an effective movement toward awakening? When has it not been necessary for a vital movement to scratch gravel by itself till it has proven its worth, when the Church "makes virtue of the faith it had denied"? Committees do not beget them. Are these inspired men part of the Church, or are only the committees part of the Church?)

2. "The visits produced rather sharp reactions pro and con." (Can you imagine anyone reading the Act of the Apostles, or studying the history of spiritual awakenings, who would be surprised at "sharp reactions pro and con"? Has the living presentation of the Gospel ever produced anything else? The same Gospel which convinces also convicts. Here is rather a badge of authenticity than a proof of unsoundness! Criticism of evangelism, as Dr. John Mackay said in this direct connection, "is in the grand tradition.")

3. "The team's lack of maturity in undertaking to deal so intimately with students' lives and souls." (What is maturity? Is it avoiding such direct work, taking refuge in organizational and intellectual approaches, or is it such power of communication that you get your message across to those who are not being touched by the usual approaches? I know one clever pagan, a complicated person psychologically, with whom one of these three men got in contact. No one in the college religious setup even knew him—he saw to it that they didn't. This man says frankly he was brought up in evil, mired in it, saw absolutely no way out of it, believed nothing and was desperate. It took the most careful and sympathetic handling, but he has come through to the beginnings of a living faith and commitment to Christ. Is this immaturity? Or is immaturity the failure even to be able to get in touch with a man like this, let alone do anything for him?)

4. "Reports on the results and follow-up were extremely varied. Where there appeared to be the best response, there occurred the least integration with the campus Christian groups." (It appears to me that this principally reveals in "the campus Christian groups" a lack of understanding of how newly converted people behave and what they need; a protective and possessive view of their own fields of work, and an impatience to secure at once some results that would come about naturally at a later stage. To expect a quick turn away from men who have brought you a

dynamic spiritual experience, to men whom you may not know and who have for one reason or another failed to introduce you to that experience, seems to me immaturity and unwisdom of the rankest kind. In time the felt need for integration with the Church and established religious forces will come about, provided those who represent these regular agencies understand what has happened to these converted people, are thankful for it, and seek to provide nurture for it, not a substitute for it.)

The blunt comment of one who knew this situation intimately was, "The gap between the impact of evangelists, and the often complete spiritual powerlessness of the incumbent on the spot to bring about such results, is so wide that in order to save his face the incumbent must deny their power."

I have given this incident in some detail because the story of the Church's dealing with men and groups who have challenged it to awakening while trying to live within its framework and being fully loyal to its doctrines is a shabby, even scandalous one. Rome's treatment of St. Francis and of the great movement he set in motion, the Church of England's ghastly mistakes concerning John Wesley and what turned out to be one of the greatest awakenings of all time—these do not make pleasant reading. We see these things in the past; when shall we have insight to see them in the present, and courage to stand behind the nascent awakening and give it backing instead of criticism? When will the Church care more for the desperate spiritual needs of the world than for its own prerogatives and little ineffective spiritual habits and prejudices? One would think that men charged with responsibility in the Church would welcome genuine awakening, and that if they do not have the awakening power themselves, they would at least be thankful when it comes from elsewhere. We seem to need to hear our Lord's clear judgment, "Ye entered not in yourselves, and them that were entering in ye hindered" (Luke 11:52).

If we had a dozen awakenings to choose from, we might have more right to be critical. But God seems to exercise some economy in the matter of awakening. With the world's need what it is, we do well to see what judgment the fresh movement may bear toward us, rather than only what judgment we may bear toward it. We may be found fighting against God. History bears out the true prophets and evangelists. In the long run, men who fought and died for true convictions are justified and honored by scholars of future generations. Why do we honor the dead prophet, and persecute or ignore the living one? Obviously because the one long gone is no present thorn in our side. Or because we are ourselves so far removed from the firsthand realities of Christian faith, and how men are converted to it in decisive ways, that we do not even recognize it. Maybe there is not even enough insight left in many of our churches and clergy to know the real thing when they see it! So we discard or attack what we fear or do not understand. It is a pitiful and deplorable situation.

The Church needs to learn what goes into awakening, what it takes. To that we address ourselves in another chapter.

VIII

Not Only

for Episcopalians

I am an Episcopalian. I am not a convert to the Episcopal Church—converts often lose their balance on coming into it. My family has belonged to the Episcopal Church in all its branches for generations. I love it. It is in my blood. I have never in my life thought of belonging to any other communion. This is in part the conservatism of accepting the familiar. It is also based on a conviction that the Episcopal Church affords potentially the widest opportunity for the various expressions of spiritual faith and life to be found anywhere, and the richest forms of worship known to Christendom. I agree with Dean Pike when he says that we are more truly Catholic than Rome, more truly Evangelical than Protestantism generally, more truly Liberal than Unitarianism.

But, as one loves his nation to no good purpose when he loves it "right or wrong," so he loves his Church to no good purpose when he does not see its faults and long to see them eradicated. For all our activity, for all our ability to commend our church to so many intelligent people, we reflect as meager a spiritual power as any body in Christendom: witness our appallingly low gifts for missions, and the fact that in spite of our wealth we are eighth in the list of total giving. Also the fact that, though we have doubled in numbers since 1900, our clergy numbers have increased only from 5,000 to 7,233. A great many of these have been accessions from other communions—fifteen hundred of our present clergy have never attended an Episcopal seminary. Many a morning congregation is a very picture of respectable futility, and the world is little affected by our having met. Many a Lenten service is a pious extra that is a substitute for spiritual power, and only confirms us in our inadequate spiritual habits.

Many a Canterbury Club is nothing more than a holding operation on a campus—the chaplain tries to capsule these students in good, Anglican paraffin when they come to college, and send them out at the other end as untouched as when they came in. I know a parish with a distinguished place in the history of our Church where there has not been a Confirmation in three years. Many Episcopalians are fond of poking rather supercilious fun at the long and too-informative sermon in many Protestant churches. Our contrast should not be with present-day Protestantism; it should be with religion in the apostolic time, with which we claim to have rather a better connection than some others do. Are we very much like the early Church? Harnack says, "The original enthusiasm evaporates, and the religion of law and form arises." Some of this is inevitable, but it should not prevent our going back to set our compasses always by the life and achievement and persecution of the early Church. Our historic antiquity is not the only basis for authenticity. There is no use talking in a Church about being "apostolic" in derivation if it is not "apostolic" in nature and result.

We are not giving our people what they need. We are giving them—and others through them—a false idea of what Christianity is. We let them off, we let them down, we fail them, and we fail our Lord. Recently I saw an old man—devout, loyal, open-minded, a churchgoer all his days. He is still looking for something he is not getting from his parish: he told me so. He seems to me as tantalized by real religion as a mule is tantalized by an ear of corn swung out on a pole over his head to coax him on. He seems to me to have been trying to get something to drink all his life through a long, Anglican straw, and to actually have been sucking mostly air. He is God-hungry, wistful, unsatisfied. He looks up and is not fed. He could have been turned into a spiritual force. Actually he has been made a kind of ecclesiastical pack horse.

Our preaching is often, perhaps usually, "over people's heads." This does not mean they do not have plenty of brains to understand our words. It means they have not grasped nor lived through in experience the earlier and more foundational steps in the Christian faith and life. One not infrequently hears a man preach a thoughtful, scholarly, well-prepared "spiritual" sermon. It falls as lifeless as a lead balloon. Half these people are church-hardened, and have no idea of changing. Some of the other half are searching but bewildered, and no one has ever given them expert individual spiritual care—only information at Confirmation. They have never got into the thing. They are spectators. Yet the preacher speaks to them as if they were striving with all their hearts to serve God and His Kingdom! Dr. Visser 't Hooft says that we are preaching to the world as if it were the Church. We desperately need foundational, arousing, converting preaching. So much of our material is way downstream, and our people are still way upstream.

Consciousness of Need

There is a widespread feeling in the Episcopal Church, as in all other churches in this startling time, that we certainly need "something." I shall never forget being at an informal clergy meeting in New York in 1948, when we were preparing for Bryan Green's astonishing mission at the Cathedral. For some months previous we had gathered about once a fortnight to prepare spiritually for the mission. The Bishop had asked me to lead these gatherings, which met usually at the Church of St. Mary the Virgin. All sorts came—High and Low, big and little, colored and white. Men opened their hearts and mouths as they seldom had a chance to do in clerical gatherings, except to debate something in convention. One day Dr. Leicester Lewis, a vigorous High Churchman and a fine scholar, musingly said aloud to us words to this effect: "We terribly need a new spiritual movement in the Church today. We have had three—the Wesleyan movement with the Evangelical emphasis, the Oxford movement with the Sacramental emphasis, and the Liberal movement with the emphasis on open-mindedness, scholarship and social application. But we need a new one. I wonder whether this is it."

We all wondered. Some of us hoped and prayed deeply. I believe myself that this might have been the beginning of spiritual awakening that could have swept the Episcopal Church. After all, New York is a tough situation, and when you can get forty-two thousand people to go to the Cathedral during a week to hear simple, dynamic preaching of the Gospel, you have a seed and a root that is alive; anything can happen. Why didn't it?

Because the effort at follow-up consisted mainly of a clergy "committee" which after a while just stopped meeting at all, and of a few parish missions conducted by clergy themselves but lacking not only the power of the great mission but also the power they might have had if the clergy had acknowledged their own need to be further converted. There were not half a dozen parishes prepared to follow up the results of the mission at the Cathedral by anything except making these new converts into just the kind of people we had already. I do submit in all frankness that even if we multiplied our two million Episcopalians by twenty, America and the world would not be a very different place unless there occurred a spiritual change as great as the numerical. A mission produces a few spiritual cut flowers; a revival (which is what we desperately need) would strike a root and grow. Our leadership was too timid, too easily deflected back into the uninspired channels, too ready to think that the only purpose of a mission was to increase the number of Confirmation candidates. So this did not produce what we had hoped for, not because Green himself was not magnificent or because the Holy Spirit was not there in power (for He was), but because the mission began only with the enlistment and cooperation, not with the conversion, of the clergy. I hear bishops lament the need of the clergy for conversion; I see mighty few of them wrestling with their men and producing it. It is so cheap for bishops and clergy to "talk spiritual."

Other Expedients

Realizing our lamentable adult ignorance, our Church has gone in for a very elaborate and expensive effort toward religious education. I am thankful for what it has accomplished. But I see only three motives that make a child go to school, or an adolescent to college: (1) pressure from the family; (2) pressure from social convention; (3) actual thirst for knowledge. In the case of religious education, the first is slight and decreases with maturity; the second hardly exists in a secular society; the third must be created by some appeal to the interests of the person involved. Otherwise, he or she will have no appetite for religious knowledge, and neither seek it nor retain it if acquired. Actually, a kind of evangelism must precede any effective religious education. For until a man comes to believe in the importance or the truth of religion, he will not care to learn the detailed facts of it. Once a person has acquired some faith, and known something about our Lord, he wants to know more. Till such time, you have not even got his attention. Here lies the terrible weakness of the present-day Church.

Another way we use to stir things up is special services, speakers, missions. These can be of immense assistance. It does us good to hear a new voice, to hear the Gospel night after night for a week or two, to be given a concentrated awareness of the power of religion. The danger is to think that public talks will accomplish what only great amounts of time poured into individuals will do. How many clergy and lay people there are who, on finishing such a mission in their parishes or returning from a conference where they have been stirred, speak with relief of "getting back to normal"! This means that, while we may have turned over in our sleep once or twice, we have not awakened. We have been given a salve when what we need is an operation.

Much more widespread in the Episcopal Church has been a turning to those beliefs and practices that are included under the appellation "high church." Men brought up in moderate parishes will go to seminary and come out talking about "the Mass" and expecting to be called "Father." They will not infrequently take parishes of evangelical or moderate position, and in every way seek to elevate them also to the "high" position and practice. If their bishop happens to be of their stripe, this practice represents a concentrated effort to "take over" the Church and move it in the same direction. Sometimes this is achieved by methods that are, to say the least, something less than honest. A parish has a personality, and sometimes this wrenching of an institution off its traditional hinges in a different direction is like trying to make a left-handed child write with his right hand. Many leave, and go quietly to a Presbyterian or Methodist Church, or silently (and I think uncourageously) allow this sort of thing to go on without protest. There is a true and valid Catholicism at the heart of the Episcopal Church in which I, like all loyal clergy of it, entirely share. But I deplore the political tactics, and the totalitarian spirit, which often characterize some of the people in the Anglo-Catholic wing of the Church.* Still more do I fear for the young men who see in a sudden turn to becoming "Catholic" the full answer to their and the Church's need.

For ours is both a Catholic and an Evangelical Church. Our clergy are ministers of the Word and of the Sacraments. Not one or the other—but both. Some people are temperamentally and by conviction Protestant, some are by the same token Catholic. Extreme Anglo-Catholics find it hard to allow for the Evangelical elements in our Church; extreme "low" churchmen find it hard to allow for the Catholic elements. As the Catholic conviction of the Church requires a right belief and Confirmation, so the Evangelical conviction of the Church requires a right experience and Conversion. But no man is a loyal communicant or priest of our Church who does not give loyalty to both these elements. It is good training in human freedom and association for us to find ourselves bound to work with men with whom, in important matters, we disagree.

I do affirm, however, that other things being equal it is easier to put on the harness of the sacramental system, to make it the be-all-and-end-all, to idolize it, than it is to work and strive to turn one's inner life over to God so deeply that spiritual power may come in and through one's life. The catholic "system" is all worked out; you learn the practices and the postures and the philosophy that go with it. I know good and saintly men for whom this is the heart and center of the Christian religion; I honor and respect them even if I do not agree with them altogether. It is when this "catholic" emphasis is made a substitute for the evangelical, even sometimes a defiant repudiation of it, that I say these men are not only missing an essential element in the Christian religion but are being extremely bad Anglicans and teaching other people to be such. It is—I say it again—an easier thing to go in for the catholic "system" with its often mechanical implications than to seek such personal consecration, personal discipline and personal power as God can use to the maximum.

---

* There are times when the "evangelicals" are just as one-sided, and one deplores this in equal measure.

Sacraments and Conversion

What the Evangelical is concerned about is the initial conversion of the soul to Christ and its subsequent upbuilding in fellowship with Him. If he be an Anglican Evangelical, he will know that this upbuilding must take place in the Church itself, and he will know the centrally important place which Baptism and Holy Communion will take in this. If he be also a strongly Catholic Evangelical (I know Catholics in our Church who are much more strongly Evangelical than some so-called Evangelicals who are way over at the other end of a thin Liberalism with really no Gospel' at all), he may also make use of other practices in the Episcopal Church which are often but mistakenly called "Sacraments." The Prayer Book (p. 292) makes it very clear that there are only two Sacraments that Christ has ordained— "Baptism and the Supper of the Lord." It also explicitly states that a Sacrament must be "ordained by Christ himself." It is perfectly clear that He ordained Baptism and Holy Communion; it is by no means clear that He ordained ordination, marriage, unction, confession, or Confirmation as Sacraments, though all these may be deducible from what He said. To regard these things as of the *nature* of Sacraments is, I think, in line with His mind and with the basic ethos of this Church. To call them "Sacraments" outright, as if they stood on a level with Baptism and Holy Communion (and this is generally done by many "high church" teachers) is, I think, disloyal both to Him and to the Prayer Book.

When you speak about conversion in a gathering of our clergy, you can feel some men bristle. They wait for you to mention the word "Sacraments," and you can see them sit more easily when you do. How many bishops take care to mention the word, as if it were a shibboleth which alone will keep the very "high" brethren happy! It is evident that they take the Sacraments as providing a kind of Anglican substitute for conversion.

To them I should like to quote two Anglican sources, the "Catholicism" of whom stands in no doubt.

Dom Gregory Dix, in his monumental work, *The Shape of the Liturgy* (p. 18), writes, "The Christian had a personal qualification for being present [i.e. at the Eucharist, baptism and confirmation]. Before receiving these sacraments he was required to make an explicit statement that he shared the *faith* of the church in the revelation and redemption by Jesus Christ." I should take this "qualification" as an indispensable spiritual condition. If he really shares in the faith of the Church, he must have been converted to Christ and have made that acknowledgment public when he was confirmed. The most mechanical of churchmen would admit, I am sure, that this represents something else than an intellectual assent to the Church's belief about Jesus: it represents a personal commitment to Him, a spiritual experience of Him. And lo! this is just what the Evangelical has been asking for all along as conversion!

Bishop Walter J. Carey is an Anglo-Catholic with fire in his heart and soul. Many years ago he wrote a book called *Conversion, Catholicism and the English Church,* in which he had this to say of the relation of conversion and Sacraments: "Sacraments come at a later stage than conversion. They are certainly equally necessary to full Christianity, but they are logically subsequent. Sacraments bind the converted to Him to whom they have been converted, but unless the conversion has taken place there is no reason why any one should ever wish to use the Sacraments." The Holy Communion is food for the Christian life, but you cannot feed a child until it begins to live! The "new life" comes first, then sustenance for it. To expose people exclusively to Sacraments without sufficient balance from the Word spoken to the heart, looking toward the ever-deepening experience of conversion, is to be disloyal to Christ and to the Episcopal Church.

Sacraments and "The Word"

There is a growing feeling in our Church that other services than Holy Communion are so inferior to it that they become almost inconsequential. This neglects part of our loyalty to a Church that believes in the Word as well as in the Sacraments. It was a devoted and learned Anglo-Catholic friend who pointed out to me a passage from St. Bernardino of Siena, one of the greatest of the fourteenth-century Franciscans, who said, "If thou canst do any one of these two things, hear the Mass, or hear a sermon, thou shouldst rather leave the Mass than the preaching, for the reason herein expressed, that there is not so much risk to thy soul in not hearing Mass as in not hearing the sermon." And this friend also told me of an English friar who wrote, in *Dives et Pauper,* "It is more profitable to hear God's word in preaching, than to hear any Mass. . . . by preaching fold be stirred to contrition, and to forsake sin and the fiend, and to love God and goodness, and be illumined to know God. . . . The virtue of the Mass standeth in the true belief of the Mass, and specially that Christ is there sacred in the Host. But that may men learn by preaching God's word and not by hearing of the Mass." In the book, *A Priest and His People,* James Wareham writes, "It can be seen from many early manuals that it was considered (in the early years of the Church and before the Reformation) as much the duty of a Christian man to hear sermons as to hear Mass, and therefore as much the duty of a Priest to preach as to minister at the altar."

The two things are complementary, not contradictory. We need to hear the Word which teaches, stirs, convicts, and—when powerful—converts the soul. We need to feed upon our Lord Himself in the Holy Communion that what has been begun may be continued. To go on practicing the sacramental life of the Church as if one had been converted to Christ, when all he has been converted to is the beauty or order or sacraments of the Anglican Communion, is simply a form of idolatry and needs to be called such. Our seminaries are full of young men who need to hear this truth. Many men long in the ministry are forgetting it. Thousands of our communicants are being misled, not because the Sacraments are not of tremendous importance, but because conversion and the direct obedience to our Lord is also of tremendous importance and they are not being told these things. Our churches are filled with communicants some of whom know what they are doing and are beautifully ready for what they receive at the altar, and some of whom need like everything to hear a convicting word that will lash their souls into revolt and then into penitence. I know a pious old fraud, sour at home, proud everywhere, soft on himself as melted butter, who goes to Communion with terrible regularity. He avoids the "word" which he needs much more than he needs Holy Communion *at this stage.* Holy Communion will be wonderful for him when he gets converted. Such people (and all of us are like that sometimes) prove that there is nothing automatic nor necessarily evangelizing about Holy Communion. We need the Word of power speaking directly to our souls, in preaching, in personal witness from others, and straight from the Holy Spirit Himself. There is no substitute for these.

What Will Shake the Episcopal Church Awake?

The answer to this question lies, of course, in the secret counsels of the Holy Spirit Himself. Only He can do it. He needs instruments, however, and these we might do something to provide.

I do not believe that the answer lies in tighter and tighter companies bound together by "churchmanship." I deplore the organized, sectarian assault being made on the Church by some of the Anglo-Catholics. I should equally deplore an organized, sectarian effort on the part of the Evangelicals. Divisive and partisan plans do not make for the health and power of the Church. What we need is something far deeper than any of this. We need a far truer "evangelism" that may have both Evangelical and Catholic elements in it, but "evangelism" always sounds emotional and transient. Often it is. We have made some considerable efforts at evangelism in our Church of recent years, and have to admit that, even in the Episcopal Church where we are aware of these dangers, we have thought that the spurt was all there was to evangelism. I am often charged with thinking this myself, but this is not the case! The rousing beginnings are greatly needed to wake us from sleep, from lethargy, from mediocrity, from spiritual halfheartedness. But what we need is much more like a determined revolution than a temporary revival.

What we really need is the conversion of the Episcopal Church from top to bottom, beginning with our bishops, going right through our clergy, and all our people. We do not need the temporary awakenings we have sought through city or parochial missions; we need steady, powerful, continuous changing of lives on the part of every bishop, clergyman and communicant of this Church. What we potentially *have* in our Church is wonderful. What we *do* with what we have is almost disgusting. We are growing more slowly than Rome, more slowly than most of the Protestant communions. Our giving is scandalous. We need genuine revolution, of spirit and of methods. We shall not get it by short-lived dissatisfaction nor by short-lived resolutions. It could happen, but I am quite sure that it will not unless we stop dead in our tracks, realize that all our suggested nostrums and panaceas are simply too shallow, too cheap, too remote from the deep needs of our hearts to produce any such thing.

The spiritual revolutionizing of the Episcopal Church might let loose a flood of power that would sweep the world. I submit that nothing so demands the attention of our House of Bishops as this, no business they have to transact which can compare to it for importance. I call on them, with all respect but also with all urgency, to take up the challenge which these facts lay before them.

IX

What Awakening

Takes

An intelligent and devout layman, who has always seen the faults of the Church, but longs to see it carry Christian belief and power to its people, said to me one day when we were being honest about where the Church falls down, "And yet, we must have it—there must be something permanent to carry all this, must there not?" "Yes," I said, "we must have the permanent, and we must have the reform also. I believe that God gives us not only a Church, but also the Holy Spirit within the Church to stir and change and awaken it lest it die of its own customs."

This reformation should be continual. When the lights burn low, we call in experts to turn them up for us—but we ought to be doing this all the time ourselves. Special missions and evangelistic campaigns are like blood transfusions; they may be very necessary when the body is ailing. If the body cannot make its own blood, it must get some from elsewhere. But it ought to be making its own blood! Every minister, every concerned layman, every parish, ought to be continuously engaged in awakening. "Lord, revive thy Church, beginning with me!"

How Awakening Begins

Awakening does not start because a committee thinks that it would be a good idea. It begins usually in the depths of the life of a man whom God has chosen and endowed for this kind of work. There are many more such men than ever get under way, because not enough men in the Church give themselves with abandon to God, and find out all that He wants them to do. Such a man must himself first be converted, find Christ, come into spiritual power.

Often he has had a lifelong spiritual exposure to the things of the Spirit. But somewhere these must become *his own*. That may happen when he comes in contact with another person who is truly in touch with God, gives evidence of it in his own life, and provides both the channel and the challenge that are needed. You never can give away what you do not possess. Christ, the Gospel, the faith of the Church, must possess us first. There may be much misgiving and great spiritual struggle; somewhere there must always be a great "giving in" that abandons self-generated power for God's power.

He may be a man who flies solo, and does most of his work in public meetings by speaking. But he really needs about him a team. No one man can possibly handle dealing with all the individuals who have been touched, as the work increases. Besides, a group makes a deeper impact on people than one man ever can. There is power in the group that no one man ever possesses. So this man begins reaching out to one, two, five other people who are drawn to him by something organic, not organizational.

Oftentimes the small meeting is better than the large. Twenty or thirty people at close grips have opportunity to ask questions, to get their problems aired, to try some experiments. Here there can be informality and laughter and the human contacts that God uses. Many a man who would be incapable of handling a great meeting or service can learn to be sensitive and effective in a gathering at somebody's house. Here is infinite opportunity for the layman as well as the parson. Out of these come the personal interviews that mean conversion and new life and people who can extend the awakening.

Awakening does not take great saints, else there would seldom be awakening. But it does take a converted man or woman. One day I talked with a theological student about our need to go much further in our work than most seminaries or churches ever go. I said that we needed real Christian revolution. "How do you get that?" he asked. Five hours later he was wrestling on his knees with Christ: would he or wouldn't he let Jesus Christ really become the dominant factor in his life? Would he let go and surrender? He knew many facts; he did not yet know his Lord. And when finally he gave himself in as complete surrender as he could, the Lord came in. "I hope," he said, "that I never get any higher than I was kneeling on that floor." And I said to him, "That's where the Christian revolution begins."

A converted person, witnessing to other persons and drawing them into a living, witnessing company—that is what starts awakening.

Difference between Working and Being Used

One reason so much of our Christian effort never gets to the level of awakening is that it is *self-effort*. We are busy doing a job for God. We "put our backs into it" as we say, and pour out our energy. The better it goes, the more we find ourselves saddled with added activity, distraught with increasing details, maybe one jump ahead of a nervous breakdown. This work needs all the energy and ingenuity any man can put into it, but it cannot be done by self-effort. It is not our aim in Christ's work to make people good or to get them to do a job; it is our aim to draw them into the fellowship of sinners whom God has saved and is changing, and for all of us together to put ourselves at His disposal and ask to be *used*. We are not originators or starters; we are channels and carriers. A wire does not need to suck power from a dynamo; it only needs to be brought in touch with it. God uses all the people He can touch. Our willfulness and self-effort stand in His way as much as any of our other sins. "Lie low in the Lord's power," said Emerson. Pray all the time. Pray that you will be used this day when you get up in the morning. It will surprise you how much begins to happen when you stop trying to do a job for God, and just let God work through you.

"An Intense Preoccupation with Individuals"

I believe that the greatest unwritten portion of the Gospels is the time Jesus spent with individual disciples. It is almost impossible to imagine His having instilled so much into the Twelve unless He gave a great deal of time to them individually. Like medicine, you can talk about general things in religion, but when it comes to application, you must deal with the relevant factors in the situation of one individual at a time. So much of the work of the churches is in companies and "wholesale." The deepest and most important work is always with individuals, hearing their stories, going out to them in understanding, helping them to see where Christ can make all the difference. I knew a deaconess in the Episcopal Church who became soundly changed after many years in her work. One day she had lunch with a woman in the parish where she worked, and after two hours that woman made a definite decision for Christ. The deaconess, with joy in her soul, reported this to the rector. What do you think he said? "Two hours for one woman? You could have called on eight people in two hours!" What ghastly failure to realize what it takes to get people deeply changed and related to God! That man had absolutely no idea what must go into winning one person to the place where he or she can win others. We need what Harold Begbie once called "an intense preoccupation with individuals." Random talks, short talks, long talks, talks that "happen" and talks that are planned—that is what we must catch if we are to move past the secularized committee work and organizational detail wherein so much of our so-called religious work is bogged down. If we are prepared to give time, care, prayer, self-spending for people, then—and then alone—shall we hew out the people that know what the Gospel is, commit themselves to Christ, and go to work intelligently and determinedly for and with Him.

Persons and the Gospel

We must never confuse our message with ourselves, and we must try not to let others do it. But we must not fear to take the consequences if they do. It is one of the ways God works most commonly—through persons. They become spiritual challenges to others because they represent an issue.

When one meets the issue squarely, such people become his best friends, and he is eternally loyal and grateful. Within these intimate bonds of fellowship God often forges the groups and teams that He can best use. We must not make God out of these people; they still remain fallible and sinful as we do: but so long as they stay in the truth to which they introduced us, we owe a kind of obligation to them and to the Spirit who used them, to be loyal. We must not become "party" people, but we must be loyal ones. St. Paul is frank with the Corinthians about others who come in with modifications of his message, "Though ye have ten thousand instructors in Christ, ye have not many fathers: for in Christ Jesus I have begotten you through the gospel. Wherefore I beseech you, be ye followers of me." Doubtless St. Paul can say that better than we; but there is timeless truth here about the way God intends to use people to reach people.

How People Behave under Conviction

A different situation arises, however, when anyone refuses to face the issue and challenge which another represents. The Gospel asks for a verdict. So do the men who truly represent the Gospel. We like to evaluate these men, say whether we like them or not—but all the while the thing they are saying estimates and judges us, and we know it. Everybody knows that the challenge of Christ-centered living asks of people something that stirs them to the depths. If they meet it with honesty and humility, well and good, but if they meet it with refusal and rejection, trouble brews. You then get the stung and convicted conscience. The Church as a whole too little understands what people do when they are under conviction of sin.

For one thing, they lie. They exaggerate the faults and misrepresent the ideas of those who have challenged them. One can hear the most fantastic reports, having no resemblance to the truth, about people who bring the spiritual challenge to others. They are of a piece with the reports that the early Christians were "cannibals" because they ate the Body and drank the Blood of Christ in Holy Communion! Rumors and lies fly about concerning how they get their money, their personal lives, their mistaken methods. I heard it confidently said that the young men who composed the team I spoke of in the last chapter encouraged the wildest public confessions, and always wore a "uniform" of light coats, gray slacks, dirty white shoes, and a red carnation in their buttonholes! All of this is whole-cloth falsehood. It is not hard to see how this comes out of the sort of ridicule which is not good-natured teasing but downright evasion of the challenge itself.

For another thing, they let each other down. A young man, let us say, finds a vital, life-transforming experience of Christ. It shakes him from his lethargy, and asks of him a commitment and level of living far beyond what he has ever known. He tries it and for a few weeks or months goes along working at it, falling down and getting up again. Then he may run across a minister or other instructed Christian in whose life this level of commitment is not even attempted, who lives on the humdrum level without miracles or much expectation. The young man asks this older Christian's advice. The advice which is given is apt to be not according to the asker's need, but according to the answerer's failure to live at such a pace and level as is now being called in question. "Well, of course I think old ——— is a wonderful fellow and we all need stirring up in the church, but at the same time I do think he asks too much of people. . . ." The end of the sentence is a tragic letdown for the young questioner who may by now be open to finding a spiritual "out." This adviser, mind you, may pray fervently for awakening in general, but when it occurs in particular, and with a challenge that comes too close to himself, he engages in the practice of letting down. An undercurrent like this can get going through the Church, can freeze up souls that were open and stop God's work in many lives. That is just what happens when an individual or a church refuses to face and accept and meet the challenges that arise right in their own midst. Some who might have been touched now feel justified in walking away. Without the courage to go directly to those who have been used to bring about this new life in someone, and ask about what they do not understand, they just pass along the questioning, negative word to people too immature to see through their own convictedness. What a waste and wreckage I have seen created by letting down! We take for honest opinion what is nothing but the self-justifying cry of a convicted heart. By such action those who should be the friends of awakening become its enemies. Jesus dealt very drastically with people like this; for evidence, read John 8, beginning at verse 12. The opposition He met was an inevitable part of the redeeming of the world. If they persecuted Him, who made no mistakes, they will certainly persecute us who are bound to make them. One who cannot face this inevitable opposition can have little part in awakening. We need to be good-natured about it, but we need to take its full measure, too. It is God they are really fighting against, not us. "He that receiveth you receiveth me, and he that receiveth me receiveth him that sent me" (Matt. 10:40).

New Wine and Old Bottles

What shall be the relation of the old organized Church to awakening? We have already seen what too often happens. The same situation existed in the relation of the new message of Jesus to the institutions of the Jewish religion. The appearance is that He made every effort to give His own people a "first refusal" on this new message. He was the Messiah, the fulfillment of their hopes and the answer to their prayers. He was nurtured on the faith of His people. It was His hope that they might "see" all this and take Him and His message for their next step in spiritual revelation and destiny. But as time went on, it became clear (1) that He was talking about something more than, and therefore in a sense something different from, the old faith; and (2) that no adaptation of the new to the old could possibly be made without taking all the reality out of the new and breaking all the customs of the old. The old arteries had hardened; if the heart pumped too fast, there would be disaster. Reluctantly (as I believe) He had this early in His ministry, and had said it plainly: "No man putteth new wine into old bottles: else the new wine doth burst the bottles, and the wine is spilled, and the bottles will be marred; but new wine must be put into new bottles." It is given by all three of the Synoptic Gospels, and it occurs early in His public work. Soon He would "call out" His apostles and set in motion something so definite that it inevitably became not a continuation of the Jewish synagogue, but the beginnings of the Christian Church.

What does this mean for us? John Wesley did his best to stay in the Church of England; in fact he never left it. But should he attempt to adapt what God was giving the world through him to the stiff, arthritic ways of the eighteenth-century church? It simply could not be done. You could not stuff the early and vital Methodism into a dry Anglican skin. It would have taken an unheard-of and practically impossible revolution on the part of the Church. Wonderful if it could have happened. But the Spirit was at work. "The wind bloweth where it listeth . . . so is every one that is born of the Spirit." I sometimes wonder what Jesus would think of our almost idolatrous loyalty to a Church that often misses completely what He wanted His people to be and to do in the world! We make a thousand excuses for it, i.e., for ourselves, and erect elaborate theories of it to justify our excuses. What it needs is nothing less than the fresh invasion of the Spirit, an awakening.

New Movements in the Church

Sometimes the Church is humble and far-sighted enough either to accept the new spirit when it appears, or to incorporate it later as part of the Church's life and work. There exists a tension here. It appears that nearly every movement of the Holy Spirit is more vital near its beginning, while it is misunderstood and not accepted, and tends to lose edge and power as it is "taken over" by the Church. Corrective as to doctrine, ministering the "means of grace," must come from the Church to the new movement. New life must come into the Church from the movement. It appears that a movement, if genuine, ought to keep to its purpose and retain some identity lest this swallowing-up process kill what God meant to do through it. There is almost always a compromise when people genuinely converted and devoted to God, who have been used to start something spontaneous and vital, allow themselves to be appropriated by the rest of the Church. They need to allow for what is given through the Church in its organized capacity, and the Church in its organized capacity needs to allow for what is given directly by the Spirit. We may expect some misunderstanding, and some difficulty. We have a right to expect of the organized Church that it have some spiritual insight, and recognize what is clearly from God, and admit that this, too, is an organic part of the life of the Church.

I think we may say that the Church on its organized side must be allowed to be watchful and on guard—conservative in the right sense. But by the time an informal movement has grown "conservative," its usefulness is probably over. The most backward-looking, out-of-date thing in the world is the radical movement become respectable. Most of us understand a formal Church, but a formal informal group is as contradictory as it sounds. Many a student movement that was born in fire today lies in ashes, and ought to be decently interred. The old organized Church, for all the stiffness of its joints, will have a more comprehensive view than such a dying movement. We need to be rid of half a dozen dead movements today, with something else to take their places.

This Is Every Christian's Business

Every Christian ought to be a center of radiating life and power and compassion. Up to the limits of his capacity, this is true of every one of the Church's members. It is not too much to expect that every Christian should: 1. Know who Jesus Christ is; 2. Be converted to Jesus Christ through an act of dedication; 3. Be able to articulate that experience for the benefit of others; 4. Be able to relate that experience to the needs of individuals; 5. Be able to relate that faith to situations, e.g., in business, etc. All it really takes is some imagination and determination and prayer.

I think of a girl in college who one morning sat down to breakfast in the cafeteria with five other girls. She is a Christian, and bowed her head in thanksgiving. The others snickered. When she raised her head, she asked good-naturedly but firmly, "What were you girls laughing at?" They said, "You know." "Aren't you grateful?" she asked. "Grateful for what?" they replied. "Grateful for the food," she said. "Why, we bought it!" they answered. "Where'd you get the money?" she queried. "Family," they answered. "Where'd they get it?" she asked. "Worked for it," they said. "Where'd they get the power to work?" she asked. She finally pushed it all back to God, and they admitted there must be a God. That evening they met again at the table. Two others said grace. Next evening, all six of them said grace. And finally she got the whole crowd into a continuing prayer group that is learning how to find and channel spiritual power! Tens of thousands of people could be doing that. Many are. But many also fall below any such expectation.

Is This Normal Living?

Is it asking too much to expect ordinary people to live like this all the time? Dick Sheppard, once vicar of St. Martin-in-the Fields London, said that "Pentecost is normal Christianity." It is normal to have people's lives so invaded by the power of God that they are lifted clear out of themselves into another kind of life in Christ. It is normal to have the fire and stir and excitement that were in the early Church. This means that, far from *average* Christianity being *normal* Christianity, it is distinctly subnormal. Someone said that the ordinary Christian's blood pressure is so low that when it becomes normal he thinks he has a fever! What passes for Christianity is a kind of cultural hangover from a Christianity that was strong enough to change people's lives, but it is distinctly no substitute for the real thing. Christianity where we are in touch with God and being used daily by God is normal Christianity. Anything less is counterfeit. There are enough people of sufficiently different backgrounds and temperaments who are living this way for us to be sure that it is universal in its challenge. There is always a kind of "stir" where the Spirit is really at work. It is conspicuously lacking in too many places in the Church today.

How About Lapses?

We all have lapses, because we are all continuing sinners. Even if we are as fully "converted" as we can let ourselves be (who of us is quite that?), we are certainly not yet fully "sanctified." The conversion may come as a crisis, the santification is always a process. Within that process there are ups and downs. The person who thinks he never has any lapses is so fooled about himself and so full of pride that he is always living in a state of unrecognized lapse. We are sometimes careless about our devotions, we lose our tempers, we won't apologize to somebody who deserves apology from us, we have frozen solid somewhere deep down and don't mean to change any more. This is lapse and backsliding on a formidable scale. And who of us has not known it? All this is as sadly and unalterably true of myself as of anybody in the world. If we try to live for God with a bang, we go off the beam with a bang—like Mayor LaGuardia who said, "When I make a mistake, I make a beaut!" But I know that normal Christianity is still the lively and expectant kind. I do not want my lapse to cool my ardor or lower my sights, only to cool my judgment of others and lower my pride. The failures have nothing to do with the validity of the times in grace. The stodgy, inactive, unrewarding, ineffective, frustrating kind of thing that passes for much of church membership is the greatest counterfeit ever palmed off on an unsuspecting humanity. Other people get the idea that this is all there is to Christianity. What was meant to be a stir, a vibrancy, and a contagion is just a routine, a habit, and a fraud.

"Maintain the Glow"

When talking with the younger marrieds one evening about eight months after most of them had gotten started, I was asked about keeping the "glow" all the time. I told them I thought a relationship with Christ was like marriage. For a while during engagement and the early part of marriage, there is a kind of wild excitement; the sight or thought of the beloved sends a person's blood pressure up and his heart beats faster. A few years after, this is not usually the case. Sometimes it is; not long ago a woman in my parish whose husband was ill, and who has been married very nearly fifty years, said to me, "I've been through a bad time over him; you see, I am hopelessly in love with him!" But that kind of devotion is uncommon. The norm here is perhaps not less love but a different kind of love. The joy and reality is no less, but maybe the excitement is. This satisfied some of them, but one of them said to me with humor in his eye, "The thing that bothers some of us is that, with you, it all seems as if you were spiritually still in the engagement period!" We all laughed, and I told them I go through my "times" like everybody else. But as soon as we admit it to God, and pray, the power goes on again. And when the power is flowing, I suppose it is always the "engagement period" kind of experience. The wonder of God is always the wonder of God. The last time it came it was as wonderful as the very first. The quiet prayer through which someone finds release in forgiveness is just as amazing as the first time a pagan turned to Christ.

Our Need for Rigorous Training

Recently a young man in my parish went downtown, enlisted in the armed services, and came back to settle final matters. I thought how like the average Christian he was—enlisted but not mobilized—his name down, his oath given, but no action, no war. Recently I asked the president of one of the greatest steel companies in the world how long he trained their field representatives. He said, "Two years." I asked myself how many Christians have ever had two months, or two weeks, or even two days, of training in acquiring and passing on spiritual power.

Set over against this the following editorial which appeared some time ago in *The Living Church:*

What would our young people think if they were asked to attend a six-month special training course in Christian life and doctrine, like the school thus described in a recent issue of the Commonweal?

"The young people, boys and girls, get up at 4 A.M., winter and summer alike. They wash in the open air, and then do some physical drill. They are then divided into small groups (of not more than eleven persons) in which they meditate on . . . doctrine and discuss pertinent questions. Silence is compulsory apart from the discussion.

"At noon they break their fast with a frugal meal, taken hastily, standing or sitting on benches. The work, done in common, of cleaning the establishment, follows. The rest of the afternoon is spent in sports, singing, folk-dancing, and lectures. Supper, another frugal meal, is again taken hastily. At 9 P.M. the 'great silence' begins, which must be kept until the following morning.

"Nobody is allowed out during the day except for half a day on Sundays. They may not receive visitors except for half an hour.

"Along with this harsh physical discipline there is a mental training almost as gruesome. Students have to accuse themselves of their faults in public and have to take humbly the accusations made by others. . . . If they misbehave, for instance, if they talk during the 'great silence' period, or smoke, they are publicly punished and even expelled."

What is this school? . . .

It is a training program for Communist youth in China. The doctrine they study is Marxist-Leninist doctrine. The missionary work for which they are preparing themselves is the organization of Communist cells in factories or schools. . . .

The Ultimate Objective

The Christian movement has always been a minority movement. There are passengers and hangers-on to this movement, but its center is men and women with fire in their souls—fire of faith and conviction that come from God, fire of compassion and concern that reach out toward men. The reason the Communist movement has made such frightful headway, taking over fifteen nations since the war without firing a single Russian shot, is that they have a philosophy, a plan and a passion for the capture of the world. They have put all this down with perfect candor, just as Hitler did: their schedule is so fantastic that our free and easy West writes it off as theoretical and goes on its way. But it is not theoretical. It is the most determined, relentless movement for the capture of the world that history has ever seen, and it has made perfectly alarming strides toward its goal. We thought once that Asia was a weedy field that would lie there exposed till we came and seeded it with Christian faith. Another has moved in now, and is sowing the field with a very different kind of seed. We shall probably see no diminishing of this revolutionary program in our time.

Christianity must have a program as dynamic, as revolutionary —one which aims at providing for the elemental needs of people's bodies and minds and souls. The world's unfortunates constitute our supreme opportunity to spread our Christian belief through the sacrament of Christian caring. The gigantic need of millions for life's necessities is our opportunity to go with skills, with faith and with compassion. Whether they will go the Communist way or go the Christian way depends largely on what we Christians do in the next five years. They know, as we do, that poverty, disease, hunger and ignorance are no longer necessary anywhere, that if they have the know-how they can lift their level of living. This seems to me to be our first priority today.

But *how* this is done may be quite as important as that it *be* done. Unless real compassion and understanding animate the people who go, they will give off a superior air. Unless humility suffuses their whole approach, their gift will be received but they will not be—and "the gift without the giver is bare." Unless faith —the dynamic, life-giving, love-giving faith of Jesus Christ—is the mainspring of all this, the whole thing will lack the sustaining power it needs. Men do not give themselves greatly except for a great motive. Loyalty to Jesus has caused more heroic and selfless living than any other motive known to history. This is why there is a direct correlation between the spread of personal faith and the spread of those deeds of helpfulness which make faith's most attractive touch with spiritual power. Men trained in practical ways of working, all living at a revolutionary level of concern and in great concerted action with one another—this is our means to the ultimate objective, that the Kingdoms of this world shall become the Kingdom of our Lord and of His Christ!

Envoi—How, for Me?

A wise and spiritual friend of mine read this far in the book and then said, "Now tell me how I get started on this personally. Put it in the simplest of terms."

The first thing is that something must happen between you and Christ. We shall never be channels of spiritual power into the world until that power has swept through us like fire through a coal. Surrender yourself to Him in concrete, specific words. It may help to seal it if you talk out just what your surrender involves with some other human being whom you can trust, and have him with you as a witness when you make this surrender. Give Him the places where emotion is active—fear, resistance, resentment, affections, ambitions. Drop the old pictures of yourself, either as unable to do anything for Him, or as merely ambitious to do great things. If we are to channel His power, something in us must break. Christ does not break us cruelly as events sometimes do (although He may be in the event for good). He breaks the pride and willfulness in us by letting us see as much of ourselves as we can "take," and then surrendering as much of ourselves as we see. I know no human being with spiritual power who did not at some point have to let go of as much as he or she saw, in as complete a surrender as was possible at the time.

The second thing is that something must happen between you and some of Christ's people. You will need a team of other people with whom to work if you are going to get anywhere. Where will you find them? Seldom ready-made. Maybe you will have to help create them. If you go to a church that is at all on fire, you may find some of them there; if it runs on purely institutional lines, you probably won't find them. But as you pray for such brothers in the spirit, they will either appear, seeking the same thing as yourself; or you will be led to them in the ordinary course of living. People like this have a way of "finding" one another as quicksilver runs together on a table top. This new thing called faith gives you a new expectation and a new imagination. You may find these spiritual partners among people you already know. It takes more than one stick to build a fire, and it takes more than one person to create a spiritual fire. A small group, like-minded, ready to pray and ready to work, is the nucleus that God is able to use.

The third thing is that something must happen, through you and these people who are associated with you, in the places where you work and to the people with whom you come in contact. Don't try to "organize" anything. Pray for open doors. Be patient where you were hasty. Be prayerful where you used to make decisions on your own. Be ready to go the second mile with the people in the office. Let the gladness in your heart come out in your conversation, in greater relaxation, in better understanding of others. Let people know you are trying to live on a new basis. Tell them what it is, when they begin to ask. Draw them into it gradually. Don't talk as if you knew all the answers, or had become a saint or a prophet overnight. If you have been religious a long time, but have only recently even thought about trying to channel any spiritual power, be honest about it; it will not be new to them that you were not very convincing before, but it will interest them that you realize it now. They are much more likely to join you in a venture that is as new for you as it is for them. Situations will change as you begin to help people to change, beginning with yourself. You will take hold of the larger world through those portions of it that you touch in daily living and work.

These three simple things are foundational to awakening—A change of heart, a company with the same purpose, an outreach to situations and people. Read all you can find on this kind of thing. Dig into your Bible with intensity. Seek everything you can learn and receive through the Church. Above all, pray without ceasing. And remember, there are thousands like you all over the world, thousands of small groups like yours, too, set on the same ends, following the same Lord. A life on fire, a group together and determined, and steady witness by the way you live and by what you say—these have always been what God could use to cause an awakening. It was the way of Christ Himself. It has been the way of every real prophet and awakener in Christian history. It is the simple, yet often costly, addition that every church must make to its routine programs. The kind of power represented by it is as available to us as the air we breathe. The church ought to give the lead in this, and its first converts must be its own ministers and members. When they know their need, admit it, and let Christ meet it, they will have an appeal for the world outside they have never had before. Give us enough individuals deciding, praying, and banding together in this way, and we shall get a converted church. And only a really converted church can do anything about getting a converted world.

And one last word—please don't put this book down, if it has said anything at all to you, without vowing to God that you will be one whom He can count on, and use. Keep praying. And it is bound to happen—by the power of God!